THE SOBER CATHOLIC WAY

Paul Sofranko

2

To Garry

1958-2019

(Thanks for seeing something in me others didn't.
We were those people who normally would not mix.)

and

to Erika

1987-2023

(Thank you for your friendship and encouragement
and knowing the right thing to say.)

Table of Contents

Preface

Welcome to the "Sober Catholic Way," a book on the many ways the Catholic Faith can assist people in maintaining their sobriety. This "Way" is my personal viewpoint and is based on my blog, SoberCatholic.com, which I began in January 2007.

The idea for the book germinated one day after I was reviewing its posts. I realized that I hadn't thought or done much about many of the things I had written about. This culminated in the realization that I have not always practiced what I've been "preaching" and therefore thought it might do me some good to organize much of the material into a coherent form that would help me reduce my hypocrisy. Seconds later I decided it might make for a nice book to publish and take its place next to my earlier Catholic recovery devotionals, "The Recovery Rosary: Reflections for Alcoholics and Addicts" and "The Stations of the Cross for Alcoholics."

Who am I? Only someone who has been sober (so far) for over two decades. I'm not boasting, hence the inclusion of the "so far." When it became obvious that my drinking was a problem, I was introduced to a popular recovery program (Alcoholics Anonymous, or "AA") which provided some initial direction.

I was not enamored with AA. I was not an honor student for early sobriety. I used meeting attendance as an excuse to pick up "supplies" at a liquor store since I had no other reason to leave the house. I felt embarrassed to be at meetings. That gradually disappeared when I began to discern the courage of those willing to share their personal stories of getting sober. However, I felt vulnerable in sharing, which caused me problems. Since I was anxious that I might have to speak in front of people, which I didn't know at first was not required, I drank for courage before meetings and again afterward to recover. Even when I discovered that I didn't have to share at meetings, I continued to drink before and after because I was an alcoholic: I drank because it was a great meeting, I drank because it was a lousy meeting, I drank because I shared something that was well-received, I drank because I slurred my words when saying how great the program worked. You get the idea…

But when I wasn't so drunk that my higher reasoning functions weren't too impaired, I paid attention and read the literature. I decided that while AA might work for a lot of people, I doubt it could be the only thing that could save me from the drink. My gut feelings said that I required more help than AA was capable of giving. I thought of it as being on the shallow end of the spiritual pool and wouldn't work as well for me. This may have been pride talking as many others have felt the same way only to their deep chagrin. However, my experiences with face-to-face and online recovery have not changed my mind in these twenty-plus years of sobriety. The Twelve Steps have helped me and have been an important part of my spiritual toolkit. However, they are not the most important part.

A passage in AA's basic text advises that we should reconsider the religion of our youth. So, with that endorsement, I figured that I'd try and see what Catholicism had to offer.

The problem was that I had left the Church about 14 years earlier and preferred not to return.

However, certain things were at stake and I started paying attention to what was going on at Mass. (I had to attend as I had been living with my Mom and she needed a ride; plus, I didn't have the heart to tell her I didn't want to go.) I tried to listen to what the priest was saying during the homilies, but nothing much came of that. I bet you were thinking I heard some homilies that "spoke directly to me" or some other inspirational bit and I was changed forever. No. Perhaps a few did, but that was most likely the alcohol I imbibed before Mass. Or, they did, but the alcohol I drank after Mass helped me to forget the important points.

I suppose that God decided I needed to be a captive audience. The consequences of still drinking after seven months of meeting attendance were building. I was making a total fool of myself in meetings (I wasn't just slurring my words during sharing, I also fell asleep, too.) My sponsor even told me that our Home Group was considering banning me on the basis that I did not have a desire to stop drinking and was becoming a distraction. Then I became physically unable to go places: meetings, Mass, liquor stores… I was often semi-conscious while on the living room couch and had no options but to watch the Daily Mass from EWTN, along with other programming that my Mom had on the TV.

Ideas slowly sank into my alcohol-softened brain. I credit Mother Angelica and EWTN with putting me on the path to sobriety. I had learned much about Catholic teachings from EWTN, and I decided to apply myself to learning more since they made sense.

I began to pray every day, including the daily Rosary. My Mom also taught me the Divine Mercy Chaplet. She made it a point to have the Chaplet recitation on TV every day at 3 PM. Plus, we had watched EWTN's Divine Mercy Sunday programming live every year together before I stopped drinking, so seeds were planted long before I needed their fruits.

I know that many people have gotten sober through AA, including countless Catholics and other Christians. But not everyone. A brief digression: if you do an online search for the success rate of AA, you'll find various studies that cite conflicting results, but all have one thing in common: it's less than half. This means that anywhere from 5-10% succeed in getting sober, with others citing a higher success rate, but still what many regard as a "failing grade." Interpret your search results in any way you prefer. It is common, from my own experience at meetings and in witnessing debates online, that the failure of anyone to get sober through AA is largely blamed on the person who tried, rather than the AA program itself. This may be accurate in a lot of cases, but it also ignores certain inherent problems of AA which might be issues at the local level, how people enter "the rooms" of AA and their unique personal background, and how that relates to AA. This is the inconvenient and uncomfortable truth of AA: many get sober through it, but many more do not; these latter either find sobriety elsewhere or not at all.

Maybe there were other reasons why I had to find a Catholic solution, perhaps alcoholism was just a symptom of deeper troubles. Religion is not a recovery program but it could help reorient the direction of one's life. Just ask anyone who has led a sinful life until they "found God." In early Twelve Step meetings of the 1930s, members read from the Bible and used Christian prayers (they still do as to the latter, namely the Lord's Prayer.) So, religion is not alien to helping with mental health and addiction issues. But often enough, one does need something to address the specific problems of alcoholism. AA (or some other program, but I have no personal experience with non-AA recovery) could be helpful when I needed to arrest the impulse to drink and it has served me in this manner rather well. The Twelve Steps are useful for providing a basic framework upon which to rebuild a life without the need for drinking. But, use the Twelve Steps as the primary basis for living and the be-all and end-all of life? No. As an extra tool when specifically needed for what it is good at? Certainly! (See: "Appendix A: Should a Catholic attend AA meetings? I heard they're bad…")

But life happens and what was I going to do about that?

So, after a fashion when I did amass some real sobriety and could remember things, I delved deeper into what the religion of my youth, Catholicism, could do for me.

One fruit of that search is the blog I started, SoberCatholic.com. I had found little from online Catholicism that directly helped alcoholics. There is the Calix Society, but despite being founded in the 1940s, it barely exists across the landscape of diocesan life in the United States. There were no interactive sites like forums particular to alcoholism recovery and Catholicism, and very few blogs and these were primarily about their personal journey and miscellaneous irrelevant topics. So, I began SoberCatholic.com to serve a need I felt wasn't being addressed: to help Catholics with addictions discover what the Church offers for them and also to help "keep them Catholic."

I had seen many Catholics leave the Church due to exposure to AA spirituality. Many weren't strong Catholics to begin with, weak in their Faith they drifted away, being affected by the moral relativism and indifferentism that pervades society, including AA Home Groups. SoberCatholic.com hopes to stem the tide, even in a small way. There are numerous Christian-based recovery programs out there, and I deem some of them to be responsible for many Catholics leaving the Faith. While they have helped people recover from the drink and the drug, they incur greater damage to the soul by removing people from the Sacraments.

Along the way, I discovered devotions, saint's writings, and numerous other things. I studied and read a lot, always keeping an eye on their value for addiction recovery. From all that, I gradually began to cobble together something like a "Sober Catholic Way to Sobriety" and wrote about it on the blog.

This book, "The Sober Catholic Way," is a summary of much of that work. The Sober Catholic Way is essentially:

Go to Mass and live the Sacramental life of the Church.

Adore Jesus in the Blessed Sacrament, possibly with frequent visits.

Study the Bible, making sure it is a Catholic one.

Study the Catechism.

Read the "Imitation of Christ" by Thomas a Kempis.

Devotion to the Sacred Heart of Jesus and the Immaculate Heart of Mary.

Say the Rosary Every Day

Consecrate Yourself to Mary

Pray the Stations of the Cross

Read The Lives Of The Saints

Get to know St. Joseph

Live the Beatitudes

Live the Little Way of St. Therese

Live the Divine Mercy Message

Live the Message of Guadalupe

Live the Message of Lourdes

Live the Message of Fatima

Live the Matt Talbot Way

That's a long list! Isn't a Twelve-Step program simpler? Perhaps. But doing the above (or trying to) has kept me sober for over 20 years when I knew that AA couldn't. If you want an abbreviated version of the Sober Catholic Way, something you can easily grasp and work out the essentials, read Chapter 6: "Devotion to the Sacred Heart of Jesus and the Immaculate Heart of Mary;" Chapter 13: "Live the Little Way of St. Therese;" and Chapter 18: "Live the Matt Talbot Way."

Anyone who takes a look at that list will conclude it is simply a devout, comprehensive Catholic lifestyle. We are all supposed to go to Mass, frequent the Confessional, and live the Gospel life which is learned by studying the Bible, the Catechism, the lives of the Saints, and other spiritual writings along with a few selected devotions to assist us on our way – to help us "stay on the beam."

So be it. But what makes it a "Sober Catholic Way?"

It is a "Way," meaning a method for living. You'll notice that the word "Live" is in many of the list items and chapter titles. In addition, many seem to invoke "relationships." Doing your best to "Live" according to the list and to cultivate the "relationships" should help you maintain a healthy sobriety and keep you in God's graces.

How well do I follow "The Sober Catholic Way?" Some points, quite devoutly, others, not so much. To be honest, my researching SoberCatholic.com for material for this book was a conversion experience, almost an AA Step 4 ("…fearless and searching moral inventory…") and I kept finding where I have been remiss in practicing what I preach. I'm not a total hypocrite, but working on this book has been rather interesting. Life hasn't been perfect for me nor am I a serene, happy saint-to-be. Life isn't good at times, and I am occasionally beset with existential melancholic dread. No one is perfect and the ideal of a happy, serene Twelve Stepper eludes most of us. But as Our Lady said to St. Bernadette in the grotto at Lourdes in 1858: "I do not promise to make you happy in this world but in the next." I do my best and keep picking myself up after every fall. (Writing this book is an example of that.) The list should help me get there, and hopefully you, as well!

Some people demand happiness in this life and they often find it by avoiding suffering at all costs, while many turn to things that can only be called "addictions." It might be the typical alcohol or drug addictions or an inordinate attraction to the self, to the Internet and social media, or fandoms (pop culture like TV and movie franchises, comics, and other entertainment stuff.) Someone may not be an alcoholic or a drug addict, but I'll wager they're "addicted" to something. You'll need many tools to crowd all that stuff out, or at least keep them in their proper perspective. That is an attribute of the Sober Catholic Way. This all could be a holistic approach to dealing with life in general and addictions in particular.

There are probably other books or devotions that should be included, but this is *my* list and *my* book! St. Francis De Sales' "Introduction to the Devout Life" should be on there, but I have never read it. ("What?!?!?" "Well…") The same goes for "The Spiritual Exercises of St. Ignatius Loyola." (If/when I read them, I'll include chapters on them in a future edition of this book.) So your list might be different. Write your own book on how Catholics can use the Faith to stay sober! Just be sure to send me a copy so I can review it and maybe add it to the list of resources in any possible future edition of this book! The more Catholics there are who write about their faith and how it applies to maintaining their sobriety, the better! The challenge is on!

This book is intended to be read and then picked up again from time to time when you need a reminder or refresher. I may be a tad repetitious here and there or at least a little "charitably persuasive" if you need the occasional reinforcing when you feel wobbly in your convictions.

> Please Note: All Scripture quotes are courtesy of the Sacred Bible: Catholic Public Domain Version. See Appendix G: "Resources on Recovery" for the website.

I: Go to Mass and live the Sacramental life of the Church

The Mass is the highest form of worship Christians can offer God.

When the priest elevates the bread and wine and utters the words of consecration, he calls Jesus down from Heaven and transubstantiates them into Our Lord's Body and Blood. They cease to be ordinary matter but become in a manner not fully comprehensible to humans, the Body and Blood of Jesus Christ. Not symbolically, but Really, Truly, and Substantially, Jesus Christ (and yet retaining the form of ordinary bread and wine.)

Luke 22:19:

Then he took the bread, said the blessing, broke it, and gave it to them, saying, "This is my body, which will be given for you; do this in memory of me."

(Chapter Two goes a little further into the details of the Real Presence.)

During a Homily on some long-ago Palm Sunday, my priest mentioned the significance of the word "memory." The word used in Luke is translated as *anamnesis*. It means to "make present," to remember it so intimately that the past event "becomes present" to you. So when we celebrate the Eucharist, it is made present in our time and place, which is more than merely recalling an event in the past. You "come into" the event, it becomes real, not merely a symbol. This is what Jesus meant when he referred to the bread as his body and said that we were to do it again as if we were present in the event.

Jesus was establishing the Eucharist. The Last Supper was the first Mass. When you attend a Catholic Mass, you are as if you are present at the Last Supper, you are as if you are on Calvary, present at the Crucifixion of Jesus. The Mass is the presentation again of the Last Supper and the continuation of the Sacrifice of Jesus on Calvary, although in unbloody form. It is NOT a re-sacrifice, or a sacrificing of Jesus again, but a participation across the chasm of time and the distance of space with what happened on Calvary. The priest, acting in the person of Christ, is carrying out Jesus' command that we do this in memory of Him. We are coming into the presence of Jesus at the Last Supper and on the Cross. We are not merely re-enacting or symbolically "remembering" an event from 2,000 years ago. We are there, regardless of where the parish offering the Mass is located. And if you think of it, this "across the chasm of time and the distance of space" idea also means that you are sharing in all the Masses that are being offered now and have been offered in the past (and maybe those offered in the future, too?)

In attending Mass you not only give God the worship due Him, but you unite your prayers and intentions with all others attending Mass. We worship in communion with others.

During the Penitential Rite (*I confess to almighty God, and to you, my brothers and sisters, that I have sinned through my own fault...,* or, some invocations followed by *Lord, have Mercy, Christ, have mercy...*) venial sins are forgiven. You still need to go to Confession to satisfy the temporal punishment due to sin. But if you have any mortal sins on your soul, don't receive Holy Communion. You are committing sacrilege and you bring condemnation upon yourself. St. Paul said in his First Letter to the Corinthians, Chapter 11, verses 27-29:

> And so, whoever eats this bread, or drinks from the cup of the Lord, unworthily, shall be liable of the body and blood of the Lord.
>
> But let a man examine himself, and, in this way, let him eat from that bread, and drink from that cup.
>
> For whoever eats and drinks unworthily, eats and drinks a sentence against himself, not discerning it to be the body of the Lord.

When you receive Holy Communion, Jesus becomes a part of you. You are transformed into Him, although obviously, this depends upon the state of your soul and your level of belief and piety.

Your prayers offered at Mass are heard with greater force than at any other time. For if Catholic teaching on the Mass is true, then the Mass is where Heaven and Earth meet. Angels in Heaven worship God, and since Jesus is physically present in the form of the Eucharistic bread, angels from Heaven descend upon the church where the Mass is offered and worship the Eucharistic God. Whether the church is St. Peter's Basilica or a lonely mission chapel in the desert, Heaven unites with Earth. Therefore, when you pray in the presence of the Lord, He hears it more clearly than at any other time, to use our manner of speaking. (Yes, God hears all prayers, regardless of the person or the place. But sometimes it is more efficacious to pray with others and at Mass or in Adoration. Would you rather talk to your spouse or best friend in person, over the phone, or by text?)

Given the above, is it any wonder that with the proper preparation and understanding, the Mass is healing? All Masses are "healing Masses" given the prayers said and the events described. In my early sobriety, I went to Daily Mass and was fortunate to have holy, pious priests offer it; I felt better and knew that I received healing, at least spiritually.

How does this relate to the Sober Catholic Way? In Twelve Step groups, it is advised that members have a "Higher Power" or a "God of your understanding." For a Catholic, this is the Trinitarian God of the Bible. Specifically, the Divine Physician, Jesus. If you want to have a "Higher Power" that is not some vague, ill-defined spirit force or a god of your creation, and would rather instead meet the Real Thing, live, up close and personal, right there in the flesh (so to speak), then go to Mass. He is waiting for you there. There is no greater love or devotion you can offer to God than prayerful attendance and participation at Mass.

Make the Mass the source and summit of your prayer life. Don't just attend Mass on Sundays, many Catholic parishes offer it throughout the week. (Catholics are under an obligation to go to Mass on Sundays and Holy Days of Obligation, unless illness, weather, or other insurmountable difficulties prevent this.) Attempting to maintain regular Mass attendance, and prayerfully participating in Mass can provide a focus. It is like a summit of

"God's holy mountain" for you to climb. You will be amply rewarded.

What is your Higher Power? How does it compare to Jesus, present at the Mass?

The sacramental life of the Church centers around the Mass and the Eucharist. However, the Sacrament of Confession is also a significant part. In Confession, you present your known sins to the priest along with how often you committed them. The priest, acting in the person of Christ, absolves you of your sins and prescribes penance.

How can this not be a popular sacrament for Catholic addicts and alcoholics? You know how much you've sinned and hurt others, this is a way to clean your soul and make it as fresh and new as the day you were baptized!

I would also add that when (or if) it is offered, you make use of any opportunity to receive the Anointing of the Sick. This used to be called "Extreme Unction" or "Last Rites," but you do not have to be dying to receive it. It should not be received regularly, but only under certain circumstances (which you should look up on your own) such as before long trips, or if you are very ill (like in the hospital or confined at home from work or school.) Also, from time to time, it can be received for spiritual healing. The Anointing of the Sick provides special graces from God to strengthen you. It is not a "miracle cure" for whatever is ailing you; although I do think there have been occurrences of these, they are rare.

So, "living the sacramental life of the Church" is central to the Sober Catholic Way.

II: Adore Jesus in the Blessed Sacrament

We Catholics have a wonderful devotional practice called "Eucharistic Adoration." In thousands of Churches, Chapels, Parish Halls and so forth all around the world, there are places where the consecrated (transubstantiated) Eucharist is kept exposed in a receptacle known as a monstrance. It is common to spend 15-60 minutes every so often in prayer before the Eucharist. In some churches, it's done on a regular schedule or even all the time. This latter practice is called "Perpetual Eucharistic Adoration."

You can spend time in prayer with the Eucharistic Jesus; with Him, through Whom all things were made and through Whom all will pass through to the Father, as John writes in his Gospel; and, as stated in the Book of the Apocalypse, through Whom all things are made new again after the End of the World.

But, as some claim, isn't the Eucharist only a symbol? The Catholic Church can't seriously mean that the bread and wine are really Jesus Christ? Well, what did Jesus Himself say about this? As He said in the Sixth Chapter of John's Gospel, verses 51-58:

I am the living bread which came down from heaven; if anyone eats of this bread, he will live forever; and the bread which I shall give for the life of the world is my flesh." The Jews then disputed among themselves, saying, "How can this man give us his flesh to eat?" So Jesus said to them, "Truly, truly, I say to you, unless you eat the flesh

of the Son of man and drink his blood, you have no life in
you; he who eats my flesh and drinks my blood has eternal
life, and I will raise him up at the last day. For my flesh is
food indeed, and my blood is drink indeed. He who eats
my flesh and drinks my blood abides in me, and I in him.
As the living Father sent me, and I live because of the Father, so he who eats me will live because of me. This is the
bread which came down from heaven, not such as the fathers ate and died; he who eats this bread will live forever."

This is the "Bread of Life Discourse." Jesus is telling His
listeners that He is the "Bread of Life," the truest path to salvation
(eternal life in the Beatific Vision with God the Father). Only
through Him is the way to the Father fully revealed. And He just
happens to mention that it is His flesh that is this "Bread of Life,"
and by eating His flesh one can attain eternal life. Naturally, this
disgusts some of His listeners who cannot accept this difficult
teaching of His and so they leave.

They are disgusted because He was speaking literally, not
symbolically, and they knew this. And Jesus knew that they knew
this.

If He was speaking symbolically, they wouldn't have left;
or, if they only misunderstood, He would have corrected them. Like
the Good Shepherd going after lost sheep, He would have chased
after all those Jews and disciples of His who found the teaching
"hard" and left. Jesus easily could have said that He wasn't speaking
literally and that they were only misunderstanding Him and should

stay. But He didn't change His story to accommodate them. He did not change the Truth because it was uncomfortable or unpopular. He knew they had difficulty with His teachings and that they understood it perfectly but rejected Him anyway. He respected their free will decision and let them go.

The entire passage from the Gospel of John (Chapter 6, verses 22-71), forms the basis for the Catholic Church's Doctrine of the Real Presence of Jesus in the Eucharist. The wafer that Catholics receive during Communion is literally, and not symbolically, Jesus: Body, Blood, Soul, and Divinity. He's all there in the form of a little piece of bread. The priest utters the words at Mass which in some mysterious way humans can never completely fathom, transubstantiates (changes the substance) the bread into His Body. And yet it remains looking like bread and retains the same matter. Our finite minds cannot comprehend how this can be, it is a Divine mystery. But we have Jesus' testimony in John's Gospel that this is so.

He said it, and therefore it must be True. You are calling Jesus a liar if you claim the Eucharist is only a symbol.

If you can believe that the Second Person of the Trinity can incarnate Himself in human form as a little baby, then you should be able to believe that after His Ascension into Heaven, He left Himself behind in the form of bread.

Humans just can't make this stuff up. It would have been laughed at into oblivion 2,000 years ago. But they believed because they understood and accepted Jesus' connecting the bread and wine to His Body in a literal manner, and something about Him helped convey its truthfulness into their receptive hearts and minds. They didn't understand it, but His followers accepted it. They knew it to be a Divine mystery and thus cannot be understood completely. They trusted Jesus.

The Jesus in John 1:1-5 is the same one in John 6: 22-71. The instrument or point or singularity through which all of Creation was made is right there in the form of bread.

Knowing this must affect you. As St. Paul wrote in his Second Letter to the Corinthians in verses 16-18 of Chapter 3:

…but whenever a person turns to the Lord the veil is removed. Now the Lord is the Spirit, and where the Spirit of the Lord is, there is freedom. All of us, gazing with unveiled face on the glory of the Lord, are being transformed into the same image from glory to glory, as from the Lord who is the Spirit.

That illustrates the effect that Adoration, being in the actual physical presence of Jesus, can have on an individual.

For we are in the Real Presence of Jesus. The Body, Blood, Soul, and Divinity of Jesus Christ are there, mysteriously and inexplicably in the form of bread. When we enter into His Presence, whether it is in an Adoration Chapel or a Church, we come before the Lord. We are unveiled before Him, and we gaze into His physical form. In the presence of God, we cannot remain unchanged. We are slowly being transformed, as St. Paul wrote, into what we see. We are transformed into the image of Christ.

Do you ever feel different when you are in the presence of someone great? That by being near them you absorb some of their greatness and charisma? Who is greater than Jesus Christ, the Son of God and who is God??

So, how is this a part of the Sober Catholic Way? Here are some random thoughts that I've had while sitting in my parish's Adoration Chapel just looking at Him while He looks back at me.

You are little...the World prefers big.

You are humble... the World demands pride.

You are still... the World is fast.

You are helpless... the World honors the strong.

You are mercy... the World teaches revenge.

You are forgiveness... the World nurtures resentment.

You are quiet... the World blares noise.

You are peace...the World is at war.

You are sacred... the World is profane.

You are trust... the World is in fear.

You are meek... the World encourages arrogance.

Just sitting quietly, whether alone with Him or with others present, is enough to "set the day aright." Consider spending time in front of the Blessed Sacrament; whether He is exposed or reposed matters little. He is still there awaiting you and welcomes you no matter what.

I may have been repetitious, but given recent polls revealing that Catholics have little belief in the Real Presence, you can pardon me for beating you over the head with this: When you go to Mass or Eucharistic Adoration, Jesus is there. The same Jesus that as the Second Person of the Trinity incarnated Himself as a man, wandered about Palestine preaching and teaching and healing, the same one Who died on the Cross for us all, is there on the altar in the form of bread. The same Transcendent, Immanent, Eternal God who became a man of flesh, blood, and bone, has remained with us these past 2,000 years in the form of bread (and wine.)

How can you not become different than you were before? Why would you go anywhere else?

III: Study the Bible (Make sure it's a Catholic one!)

The Bible is the Word of God; it is the revelation of Himself to humanity. The Old Testament chronicles the millennia before the first coming of the Messiah, Jesus Christ. It contains prophecies concerning Jesus and details the relationship between God and His Chosen People, the Hebrews. This relationship has been one of fidelity and betrayal, loss and gain, punishment and honor, and is a template for everyone's relationship with God. Study the history of the Hebrew people as written in the Old Testament and you'll see yourself in it. Every bit of it is a symbol of your relationship with God. Every time you turned to other "gods," every time you lacked faith, every time you forgot the good He has done for you and complained… the list goes on. It is the story of how we ultimately crucified Jesus by our sinning.

The New Testament is all about Jesus Christ. It is taken up by the four Gospels which detail His life and teachings and by the Letters of St. Paul the Apostle, who received the Gospel message not from any person or reading, but by Jesus Himself; as well as additional letters by James, John the Evangelist, and Jude.

The Bible is also the prayerbook of the Church; the Psalms form the backbone of the Divine Office, also referred to as the Liturgy of the Hours. This is required to be prayed by the Pope down to seminarians, by religious brothers and sisters, and by secular members of religious orders. Many lay faithful also pray it (including the author.)

You can also employ the meditative practice of "Lectio Divina," the slow, prayerful reading of the Bible. One typically uses the Psalms or Gospels (but any part will do) and slowly start to read, stopping when a word or passage "jumps out at you," and then you dwell or ponder that. The point of Lectio is not to get through a certain amount of Bible passages that morning or evening. It is not part of any "Bible in a year" scheme. You often only read one verse because a word reached out and grabbed you. Then you meditate on that, invoking the Holy Spirit's help.

You must make use of a Catholic Bible. Non-Catholic versions of the Bible, even the reputedly good ones, lack numerous books the Church regards as divinely inspired; furthermore, when they contain explanatory notes concerning a passage, these will not have an interpretation that will reflect Catholic doctrines and dogmas (see Appendix C: "What are dogmas and doctrines? I heard they're straitjackets restricting our freedom.") Since Protestant and Evangelical Christians consider the Eucharist as merely a symbol (see Chapter 2) do you think their notes on John 6 will be accurate?

Here is where I make an emotional appeal to your Catholic identity and apply this to the Sober Catholic Way. (This is an example of what I said in the Preface about being "charitably persuasive.") It was the Catholic Church that compiled the Bible during the first four centuries after Christ's Resurrection. It was the Catholic Church to whom Christ entrusted His teachings and by whom the Bible is authentically interpreted. Under the influence of the Holy Spirit, it is possible that individuals can interpret the Scripture but this is hardly reliable given the multiplicity of contradictory doctrinal beliefs amongst the tens of thousands of non-

Catholic denominations. The Holy Spirit cannot be the author of all that confusion. Given the complexity of the Bible, of the fact that it was originally written in Hebrew and Greek across millennia, and originally concerned Semitic peoples in Southwest Asia; given all the cultural nuances and historical complexities, doesn't it make sense that God intended for the Scriptures to be interpreted by one authentic source to avoid confusion? As a person making use of the Catholic Faith to work out your sobriety, doctrinal error, and confusion will hardly assist you!

You cannot entrust your growth in Faith to Scriptures that do not do justice to Catholic teachings.

IV: Study the Catechism

A catechism is a summary of all the teachings of the Catholic Church. The Catechism that taught Catholics for centuries was the "Catechism of the Council of Trent," also known as "The Roman Catechism." It is still a valid source of Catholic Truth, despite being succeeded in the 1990s by the newer "Catechism of the Catholic Church."

I'd get both!

The former plugs you into the ancient traditions of the Church and may help explain why some things are done today or help you understand the material you've learned from reading the lives of the saints (See Chapter 10), and so forth. Some of it is outdated, but for the most part, it will serve as an effective way of grounding you in the traditions of the Church, much of which survives into the present.

The contemporary "Catechism of the Catholic Church" ("CCC") is a wonderful successor to the "Roman Catechism." It presents things in a manner that is accessible to modern Catholics and is an excellent antidote to the mores currently being peddled by the cultural elites as "true."

I've read it in its entirety and spot-read parts here and there; every time I come away feeling like I've ingested a healing balm and feel "deprogrammed" from what passes for modern "values."

The Catechisms help me to come away feeling more steeped in the ancient traditions of the Church. That and the truths they espouse are the very things that help me disconnect from modern society. They root you in the oldness of the Church, a Church that has withstood and outlasted empires, dictators, republics, plagues and pandemics, democracy, tyranny, and oppression. They give you the hope needed to overcome our current troubles and helps to fix your perspective knocked out of whack by the contemporary cultural chaos. Not a bad thing to hang your recovery on.

Getting grounded in the Catechisms builds your faith; your Catholicism will become stronger and you'll be more capable of resisting the challenges of the spiritualities that AA members are exposed to. These include indifferentism: the sin of thinking that it doesn't matter what you believe in, as long as you believe in something. This says that all religions are the same. Hardly! Truth cannot be equal to Falsehood!

Becoming familiar with the teachings contained in the Catechisms will safeguard you from straying from the Church when your faith is challenged or confronted. And it will be. If you experience the fellowship of the Twelve Step meetings, you might feel inclined to gradually adopt the indifferentist and (largely Protestantized/Evangelicalized) non-Catholic spirituality.

How is this important to the Sober Catholic Way? One key piece of the Sober Catholic Way is a heavy grounding in the teachings of the Catholic Church; a solid Catholic Bible and Catechism are indispensable to this. As I've stated (possibly more than once) elsewhere, I started SoberCatholic.com because I had seen too many Catholics in AA and non-denominational Christian recovery programs leave the Church; the one thing they had in common was a lack of depth to their Faith. Studying the Catechism and incorporating its teachings into your belief system can insulate you from competing philosophies. Well-armed with the tenets of the Catholic Faith after studying the Catechism, you'll be better able to resist the errors of Evangelical recovery programs and the indifferentism common to AA meetings.

V: Read the "Imitation of Christ" by Thomas a Kempis

"The Imitation of Christ" by Thomas á Kempis is a classic of late medieval spirituality. It may be an apocryphal story, but it is said that only the Bible has been read more by Catholics. In my copy, the preface cites that many a medieval monk or hermit only had the Bible, some liturgical books, and "The Imitation of Christ" in their possession.

It is a thought-provoking book that prescribes a no-nonsense approach to living a Christ-like life. The first major lesson you learn is that if you wish to understand the teachings of Jesus better, a life that is conformed to His is the best way. This makes sense; if you become more like Jesus, then His teachings will become more comprehensible. While we may not be expected to completely adopt the teachings in the book, we can at least try. Jesus rewards our sincere efforts.

The book is divided into four parts.

Book One is called "Useful Admonitions for a Spiritual Life." It starts you off on the importance of spiritual living and how to disconnect from the world. "Admonitions" means "authoritative counsel or warnings," "reprimands," and "reproaches." That may seem harsh, but we're all sinners and sometimes we need to have someone walk up to us a slap us. Kempis does that, but he means well; he has your Salvation in mind, and the World has other plans for you (and they're not always good.)

Book Two is "Admonitions Concerning Interior Things." Continuing with the theme of admonishing you, Kempis teaches you how to develop your interior life. This means getting into your soul and making it reflect the image and likeness of God better than it currently does.

Book Three is about "Of Internal Consolation." Here, Kempis switches gears and adopts the persona of Christ speaking to you. This is the longest Book of the four, and in it, Kempis's Christ persona gently leads you along the path of spiritual growth and progress. You learn much about the interior development of the soul, walking with God, growing in holiness, and shedding character defects.

Book Four is a series of chapters that are excellent meditations "Of the Blessed Sacrament."

How is this related to the Sober Catholic Way? I cannot recommend enough the importance of making a regular or occasional habit of reading "The Imitation of Christ." As I say in Chapter 13: "Live the Little Way of St. Therese," she had the book memorized. While that is hardly expected nowadays, you should read, study, and inculcate the teachings as best you can. "The Imitation of Christ" should be regarded as a manual of spiritual growth and perfection. Reading it reprograms you; if you adopt the Blessed Virgin Mary's model of contemplation, you will "ponder these things" in your heart. It will change you.

VI: Devotion to the Sacred Heart of Jesus and the Immaculate Heart of Mary

The Sacred Heart is a traditional Catholic devotion dating back centuries. It centers around Jesus' intense, sacrificial love for us and our response to that love with a burning desire for Him that sets our hearts and souls aflame. We love Him on behalf of those who don't, which is a selfless act if you think about it.

Proponents state that it is based on the Gospel account of St. John the Evangelist laying his head on Jesus' chest at the Last Supper. The contemporary Devotion began with an apparition of Jesus to St. Margaret Mary Alacoque in the 17th Century. It focuses on the human nature of Jesus (the heart long being considered the center or source of human emotion). As Jesus had become human to redeem us for our sins, the Sacred Heart of Jesus concerns the Divine Love of God for us, and the Devotion to the Sacred Heart is our love response that serves as our reparation for our sins.

We sin, we repent, and we make reparation.

The idea of using the Devotion to the Sacred Heart as a way to keep clean and sober isn't strange to anyone familiar with the Matt Talbot Way (see Chapter 18). The Sacred Heart is central to the Matt Talbot Way. It is essentially about transferring your love for your favorite chemical onto Jesus. You "give" your love for your addiction to Jesus and if you relapse you are taking the gift back. This is all done while being mindful of the reparative nature of the Sacred Heart Devotion.

The Sacred Heart of Jesus has special significance to sober alcoholics, especially to those who are knowledgeable about AA history. One of the co-founders of AA, Dr. Bob Smith, was greatly assisted in his treatment of alcoholics by a Catholic nun by the name of Sister Mary Ignatia Gavin, an administrator of St. Thomas Hospital in Akron, Ohio. After an alcoholic completed his stay at the hospital, Sister Ignatia would "award" him with a Sacred Heart Badge, as a sort of a "graduation" gift. This eventually developed into the practice of AAs receiving medallions or coins representing whatever sobriety anniversary they were celebrating (one day, thirty days, annual, etc.)

In light of this, that the Sacred Heart was chosen as a symbol of recovery is not surprising. In our recovery, we are making reparation for the sins we had committed in our addictions. We accept and respond to the love God has for us. We know we messed up and abused the gifts God had given us. But despite all of that He still loves His prodigal children and always takes us back no matter how bad the sins we'd committed. As long as we repent and try to amend our lives we are on the right path. There is no sin too great to keep God away from us. Even with mortal sins on our souls, God awaits our repenting and returning to Him.

But the Devotion as a recovery method in and of itself, apart from the connection to the Matt Talbot Way? The essential part of the Devotion is Love and Mercy. The love of Jesus and acceptance of His Mercy after we repent and ask for it. You love Jesus so much that you are willing to sacrifice for Him, and your love isn't restricted to just loving Him, but also to loving Him in the place of others who do not or will not. This is reparative love.

Loving Him in the place of those who do not mean that you are making reparations for their sins. Sounds a bit like a making of amends? But not just for your sins and character defects, but for those of others, too. As I said above, pretty selfless.

This is perfectly in keeping with St. Paul's doctrine of the Mystical Body of Christ. St. Paul wrote that all Christians are members of Christ, so that with Him, they form one Mystical Body. (1 Corinthians 12:12-31) When one suffers, all suffer. When one rejoices, all rejoice. The Sacred Heart burns with love for all members and potential members of the Mystical Body. Our acts of reparation for the sins of others help heal it.

All sin is public; you may think your sin is a private matter, but in reality, it causes harm to the Mystical Body. This is why we have to go to Confession. Even though we confess in private to the priest, the effects of the sacrament impact the Mystical Body. And this is why when we make reparation for the sins of others, as is the key part of devotion to the Sacred Heart, then the Mystical Body can be healed.

Lift one another in prayer. "Iron sharpens iron," (Proverbs 27:17.) We strengthen each other. Return the love of the Sacred Heart through acts of reparation. Making reparations for others is an act of mercy and this can only have beneficial results for ourselves. We obtain mercy for others and it gets lavished on us.

No sin is greater than God's ability to forgive it. Our repentance has to be sincere, and we have to make the best effort to amend. But no matter how evil our sins are, we can be forgiven. No matter how often we fall, we must always get right back up.

The Gospel of John 15:13 "No one has a greater love than this: that he lay down his life for his friends." While we are not literally "laying down our lives" for others, figuratively speaking, we do when we sacrifice and make reparations for the sins of others.

So, the basic working out of the devotion to the Sacred Heart, if done with a mind to keep clean and sober, is a working out of our recovery. It turns our attention off of ourselves and curbs our self-will. In doing unto others what we should have done to ourselves, charity is strengthened and we lose the need to drink and drugs.

Jesus' love for us is so intense that it supplies what is lacking in our prayers and desires. It "fixes our past," not by a manner of temporal engineering and changing that past, but by burying our sinful past in His Heart we can find redemption. The Sacred Heart Devotion, when combined with the reception of the Eucharist and visits to the Blessed Sacrament make Jesus feel less like an abstraction and more of a real live entity.

Central to the devotion is the Nine First Fridays. When Our Lord appeared to St. Margaret Mary Alacoque He had made the following 12 promises to St. Margaret Mary in favor of those who consecrate themselves to the Sacred Heart and who attend Mass and receive Holy Communion on the First Friday of each calendar month for nine consecutive months. This is to be done in a spirit of reparation for sins committed against the Sacred Heart (basically, any sin committed against the love of Jesus, such as blasphemy and sacrilege against His Name, the Sacraments, and the Church.) Although, as is written in "The Devotion to the Sacred Heart," by Fr.

John Croiset, these 12 promises are but an abbreviation of a much longer list of promises.

1. I will give them all the graces necessary in their state of life.

2. I will establish peace in their homes.

3. I will comfort them in all their afflictions.

4. I will be their secure refuge during life, and above all, in death.

5. I will bestow abundant blessings upon all their undertakings.

6. Sinners will find in My Heart the source and infinite ocean of mercy.

7. Lukewarm souls shall become fervent.

8. Fervent souls shall quickly mount to high perfection.

9. I will bless every place in which an image of My Heart is exposed and honored.

10. I will give to priests the gift of touching the most hardened hearts.

11. Those who shall promote this devotion shall have their names written in My Heart.

12. I promise you in the excessive mercy of My Heart that My all-powerful love will grant to all those who receive Holy Communion on the First Fridays in nine consecutive months the grace of final perseverance; they shall not die in My disgrace, nor without receiving their sacraments. My divine Heart shall be their safe refuge in this last moment.

The Church grants a Plenary indulgence to those who attend Mass and receive Communion in honor of The Sacred Heart of Jesus on the First Friday of each month for nine consecutive months.

Closely related to the Sacred Heart Devotion is the Devotion to the Immaculate Heart of Mary. Traditionally linked with the Sacred Heart of Jesus, it is a devotion to Mary's interior life, as exemplified by the passage from Luke 2:19:

> But Mary kept all these words, pondering them in her heart.

This is a model of contemplative action. The contemplative aspect of Christian living is often overlooked, people believe that "doing things" is a more effective way to solve problems. Prayer is often derided as a solution. However, prayer, being the uniting of our souls and hearts to God in offering Him our needs and wants, can often produce results. Denying the usefulness or efficacy of prayer is atheistic. Ask anyone whose prayers have been answered. Ask anyone who has felt different after regular praying; it's as if prayer has changed them.

Our Lady offers us a model for the prayer life. In the passage above, where "Mary kept all these words, pondering them in her heart," there is the implication that she did not understand whatever was going on, but through prayerful contemplation, grew to understand them. It is also likely that she perfectly understood them, and in prayerful contemplation offered up her gratitude and thanksgiving. Either way, she prayed and pondered upon things in her heart.

In Twelve Step programs, we are reminded that we cannot hope to always work the program perfectly and that we should focus on "spiritual progress, not perfection." Mary, however, was our race's greatest triumph, and due to her Immaculate Conception, was sinless. She is perfect (although still a finite creation.) Although we cannot hope to be just like her, we can strive to imitate her virtues and devotion to Jesus and God the Father. Prayer is one way of doing this.

If you are struggling with impurity, a devotion to the Immaculate Heart of Mary can help ease the suffering. Mary is the model of purity, by prayerfully offering up your temptations in prayer, your suffering can be eased. This may take time, given the thoroughness by which sexual impurity and deviancy are ravaging our culture.

She can be our model in our recovery life. She can help us, inspire us, and through our recitation of the daily Rosary, be the focus of our Step 11 (prayer and meditation to connect with God) work. Yes, I think the Rosary is the best way to practice Step 11 daily (in addition to whatever other prayers you may use). You can carry a Rosary about you wherever you go. It can be recited while driving or going for a walk. Difficult to do that with a Bible or prayer book.

Just like the Sacred Heart has the Nine First Fridays practice, the Immaculate Heart Devotion has "The Five First Saturdays." These were instituted at the request of Mary in 1925, during an Apparition to Lucia, one of the then-only surviving seers of Fatima.

Our Lady requested that the faithful, on the first Saturday of the month for five consecutive months:

+Go to Confession

+Receive Holy Communion

+pray the Rosary

+meditate on one of the mysteries for fifteen minutes

+all of the above in a spirit of reparation

+Confession can be eight days before or after the Saturday.

+Communion can be received in the usual ways: either at Mass, such as a Saturday morning daily Mass or the Saturday Evening Vigil Mass, or from a priest or Eucharistic Minister, or during a Communion Service. Many parishes may have such a service to assist people in fulfilling their requirements. Check around your locale at Mass Times for parishes.

Why five Saturdays?

Five first Saturdays of reparation were requested by Our Lady to atone for the five ways in which people offend the Immaculate Heart of Mary:

+attacks upon Mary's Immaculate Conception

+attacks upon her perpetual virginity

+attacks upon her Divine Maternity and the refusal to accept her as the Mother of all mankind

+for those who try to publicly implant in children's hearts indifference, contempt, and even hatred of this Immaculate Mother

+for those who insult her directly in her sacred images.

How is this related to the Sober Catholic Way? It is the heart and soul of it. The Devotion to the Sacred Heart is tied to the Eucharist; devotees often participate in Adoration if they can (See Chapter 2) and often go to Mass (See Chapter 1) more often than the obligation requires. Participating in the Immaculate Heart brings more of the sacramental life of the church into play: Confession and prayer (and the Mass!)

Therefore, in adopting the Devotions to the Sacred Heart of Jesus and the Immaculate Heart of Mary you will be efficiently and practically working out most of the Sober Catholic Way! Regarding this, it is important to note that these devotional practices shouldn't be a "one and done," meaning that you do them once and that's it. Although technically the requirements would be fulfilled, I think that in the spirit of the devotions, you should do them repeatedly. If you miss a month, don't resort to worry and frustration. If you commit yourself to doing these every month you'll eventually forget what month you're on, anyway

VII: Pray the Daily Rosary

The beads of the Rosary are links of roses to Heaven.

As I said in my book, "The Recovery Rosary: Reflections for Alcoholics and Addicts,"

The Rosary is an ancient devotion prayed by Catholics. It has been around since the year 1214 when St. Dominic introduced the Rosary in its present form. According to legend, St. Dominic received it from the Blessed Virgin Mary in an Apparition to assist his efforts in combatting sin and heresy.

The Rosary is not about the Blessed Virgin Mary as is commonly believed by those who are unfamiliar with it. It is about Jesus. In Catholic teaching, Mary points the way to Jesus. We received Him through her: she gave birth to Him; the first prophecy of Him during His life was when Simeon took Him from Mary's arms during His presentation in the Temple; His first public miracle was after her prodding (wedding feast at Cana); and she became our Mother after He gave her to his disciple John on Calvary. Mary is the path to Jesus.

It is Scriptural. The Bible is the Word of God, and Jesus is the Word of God made flesh (Incarnate), therefore the Bible is about Jesus and Jesus brings to life the Bible.

It is the one devotional practice most commonly associated with Catholics. It is the devotion that has been written about by more popes and saints than any other (except maybe the Devotion to the Sacred Heart of Jesus.) Many have declared that devotion to reciting the Rosary is a sure sign of predestination (not in the Protestant sense of the word but rather that God knows in advance who will be saved and who won't because He is omniscient and exists outside of linear time. Foreknowledge of who will be saved doesn't mean predetermination of the saved. And devotion to Mary has the advantage of bestowing greater receptivity to graces which flow to us through her; just like if you study hard in school, you are "predestined" to go to a good college.)

It has more indulgences attached to it than any other devotion. As a spiritual practice done by the laity, it exceeds virtually all others in ease of use and simplicity of manner.

It only takes about 15-20 minutes. Everyone has time for that! There is an increasing practice of reciting the entire Rosary, not just one set of Mysteries, but all three (or four of them, if you include the optional Luminous Mysteries of Pope St. John Paul II) every day. This can be broken up across the day, for example, during your morning prayer time, en route to work, lunchtime, en route home from work, and during night prayers. You can sanctify your daily mundane routines.

Do you want to know God's will for you? The Bible is a good place to start looking. Do you want a great role model for following the will of God? His Mother is perfect. By saying the Rosary you will be meditating on the Scripture that each decade of the Rosary is based on. You can nicely combine Mary's submission to God's will with direction from Sacred Scripture.

The Holy Rosary of the Blessed Virgin Mary connects you to the Mother of God; its recitation brings you closer to her and she in turn will lead you to Jesus, as all proper Marian devotions do. Maintaining the habit of the daily recitation of the Rosary places you ever more under Our Lady's Divinely Maternal protection. It enhances, if not even ensures, our salvation. (See Chapter 8: "Consecrate Yourself to Mary.") We are supposed to "Honor our Father and Mother," according to the Commandments God gave to Moses. Reciting the Rosary is one of the best ways to fulfill that Commandment. Mary is our Mother. In some significant ways, she is more our Mother than our natural birth mother is. Since Mary is the Mother of Jesus, and Jesus is the head of the Mystical Body of Christ of which we are members, then she is our mother, too, by being the Mother of that Mystical Body. Our natural birth mother birthed us into life, but Mother Mary birthed us into eternal life when we were baptized.

As a Christian, we are followers of Christ. Meditating on the mysteries of the Rosary is meditating on the life of Christ. All of the decades are taken from the Gospels (except for two, and they are implied from Scripture.) The Catholic Church truthfully says that all proper Marian devotion leads to Jesus; it should never stop with Mary. Well, then, the Rosary beads are not only links of roses to Heaven but are the ties that bind us to Jesus.

The time I spend saying the Rosary is oftentimes like a short vacation from reality. I dwell on the mysteries of each decade; sometimes they're in the forefront of my mind and other times they rest in the background. But I am swept away from whatever is going on. Even when I am saying the Sorrowful Mysteries, it is like I am telling Jesus my pains and worries. To me, it is as if Mary is holding my hand while praying.

How is this connected to the Sober Catholic Way? The Eleventh Step of AA is about "prayer and meditation" and discerning God's will. Well, the Rosary is probably the best means of doing that. There is a tangible element to it (handling and fingering the beads) that can help in rooting you to the practice, and there are built-in meditations on the life of Christ. (If you need help, there is my book, "The Recovery Rosary: Reflections for Alcoholics and Addicts.") Furthermore, praying the daily Rosary disciplines your prayer routine. Whereas you might not want or be able to partake of other devotions or prayer practices, praying the daily Rosary sets a kind of rhythm to your day, especially if you say more than one. But even if you pray just one set of Mysteries, that connects you to Mary and onward to Jesus. And the spiritual benefits that result and the graces flowing down upon you from Heaven will leave you changed.

VIII: Consecrate Yourself to Mary

If you think that the Sober Catholic Way may be too difficult or too something else, there's an easy way to get help.

Just ask Mama! Consecrate yourself to the Blessed Virgin Mary! Consecrating yourself to Mary will obtain for you the assistance of the Mother of God! How can you possibly go wrong?!

What is Marian Consecration? It is when you solemnly dedicate yourself to the Blessed Virgin Mary through reciting an Act of Consecration. There are two popular ones, that of St. Louis deMontfort and St. Maximilian Kolbe. They are essentially the same, except that St. Maximilian's adds an external evangelical dimension to deMontfort's, and Kolbe's Consecration also makes you a member of the Militia of the Immaculata (the "MI.") The MI is an International Public Association of the Faithful (don't worry about that, it's just what they call it in Rome.)

In your solemn consecration to the Blessed Mother, you offer yourself to her as her property and possession. You become hers. Your fate is in her hands. DeMontfort's method of consecration essentially leaves it at that; you are her property, slave, or whatever. This is a declaration of humility and trust in the Mother of God that she will take care of you and guide you. Kolbe adds certain language that allows Mary to use you as if you were a "paintbrush" or "pen" in her hands to bring about the Reign of the Sacred Heart of Jesus. As an MI, you are a foot soldier in Mary's Army, leading souls to Jesus in conquering the world for Christ.

Whether your consecration is by the Method of St. Louis deMontfort or the way I did it, through the Method of St. Maximilian Kolbe, your life will never be the same. Consecration is the total giving of yourself to the Blessed Mother. In St. Maximilian's way, you are giving her permission to use you: your life, health, skills, and talents, your eternity, in any way she wants so as to bring souls to Jesus. She is the best Mother anyone can have, and many saints are convinced that no soul consecrated to Our Lady will ever suffer eternal damnation. What Mama wants that for her children? By whatever means she has at her disposal, she will lead you home to God.

How is this related to the Sober Catholic Way? Easy! By placing yourself under the Blessed Mother's care, you are protected spiritually, and maybe even physically, from that which can harm you. Even if you fall (in sin) you'll have the fortitude to rise back up. Even if you were to relapse into your addiction, chances are you'd rise stronger than before.

There is quite a lot more to this that lies beyond the scope of this little book. Please take a look at the resources in Appendix G to help you learn more.

IX: Pray the Stations of the Cross

Praying the Stations of the Cross is a devotion where you are placing yourself directly into the events of Jesus' Passion and Death. There are countless saints and other spiritual writers who have encouraged people to meditate on the Passion of Our Lord. It is often recommended as being one of the most fruitful ways to sanctify yourself, grow in holiness, and bring down a torrent of graces from Heaven.

The other fruitful way is to prayerfully read and meditate on the Passion narratives of the Gospels.

As I said in my book, "The Stations of the Cross for Alcoholics:"

The Stations are an ancient devotion of the Catholic Faith, usually said in parishes during Lent. Individuals may often say them throughout the year for their spiritual development since meditating on the Passion of Our Lord is extremely beneficial and has been recommended by saints and spiritual writers for centuries.

I suggested that:

…they help sort out the pain and suffering of alcoholism and bring some help and relief.

And:

… is merely intended for spiritual growth and progress, it promises nothing more.

That's the important part of praying the Stations. It's like a story with a beginning, middle, and end; as you insert yourself into the story you become a part of it. You are an observer or bystander on the Way. You're in the crowd when Jesus meets Mary or the women of Jerusalem, and you are standing next to Veronica as she wipes Jesus' face… or maybe you are Simon of Cyrene as he is made to assist Jesus by carrying His Cross for Him.

I liken the Way to a process where you discard your old drunken self and take on a new person. This was how I approached it in my book.

As I said above, they are typically prayed during Lent. But as a people who struggle with sin, praying the Stations throughout the year will help put you where you belong: in the hands of the Merciful God. Praying them regularly will help with your humility and spiritual growth; praying them before going to Confession may help as an Examination of Conscience or assist with your contrition. If you're not where you can read a Stations of the Cross devotional, such as when you are driving or walking, there is a Stations of the Cross (or Way of the Cross) chaplet. I use that sometimes when going for a walk.

X: Read the Lives of the Saints

A saint is anyone who is in Heaven. However, we do not know exactly who is there except those whom the Catholic Church has canonized. They get this special honor because they lived a life of heroic virtue or they died a martyr.

How the Church canonizes has varied over the 2,000 years of her history and isn't all that important for this book. In her early history, anyone mentioned positively in the Bible was regarded as a saint, as were martyrs; later on, popular acclaim by the people or a general agreement amongst the bishops would be enough. If miraculous occurrences, like healings, happened around a deceased person's tomb, that might lead to popular acclamation. For most of the past 1,000 years, the Church reserved for the Pope the final decision regarding listing someone amongst the blessed in Heaven. More recently, a certain number of miracles have to attest to the person being in Heaven: God personally works miracles through the intercession of an individual of known reputation, thus attesting that they are in Heaven. In modern times, miraculous cures are the sole criteria for determining if someone is in Heaven as this employs rigorous scientific scrutiny and methodology.

But more for our purposes, a canonized saint is a person who has lived a life of heroic virtue or who became a martyr. Even in the centuries before the Church's more carefully delineated procedures for canonization, when saints were martyred or canonized by acclaim, the individual already had a reputation for a life of piety, sanctity, or heroism.

Many people mistakenly think that saints were holy and pious throughout their lives; that perhaps God had bestowed upon them certain natural gifts that made them "better" than everyone else. No! Many were quite sinful during their lives before they "found Jesus." They often still struggled with sin and temptation afterward.

How is this connected to the Sober Catholic Way? Regardless of when someone was canonized, the person fulfills the status of being the ultimate role model for people to follow. And we can certainly make use of successful role models.

These are people who were like us; they struggled against situations and things that tempted them and caused them suffering. Although they lived and died in times when the cultures and technology may have been very different from those of today, their struggles can be linked to our lives and whatever situations we are experiencing.

For example, if you suffer from alcoholism (or know someone who does, either way, it's a certainty if you're reading this book!) then reading the life story of Matt Talbot is edifying. (See Chapter 18: "Live the Matt Talbot Way.") He has not been canonized, yet, but the process has started. Nevertheless, many of us Catholic alcoholics have already "acclaimed" him as our patron saint due to his pious habits of daily Mass, devotion to the Rosary and Sacred Heart, and regular spiritual reading. The "Matt Talbot Way of Sobriety" is a recognized recovery method in which the afflicted transfers their "love of the drink" onto Jesus.

Another is St. Mark Ji Tianxiang, who was an opium addict in 19th-century China. He did not die clean, but he persevered in his faith despite being prevented from participating in the sacraments (this was due to the insufficient knowledge of addiction in the Chinese Catholic Church of his time. Alcohol and drug abuse were considered sins, and if you didn't have a firm purpose of amendment, you couldn't receive the sacraments. Since St. Mark Ji couldn't break his addiction to opium, he was considered to lack a firm purpose of amendment.) St. Mark Ji is important, especially for those who just cannot break their addiction. Even though we have access to far greater resources than he did, and our understanding is much greater, there are still those among us who remain trapped for whatever reason. He suffered from a lack of understanding and assistance, but St. Mark Ji can intercede today for those who cannot break their chains of addiction, whether to the drink or the drug. St. Mark Ji can also offer lessons to those who leave the Catholic Church because of obstacles. Many who divorce and remarry or who persist in sexual sin leave the church because they cannot receive the sacraments. They go to a "more accepting" denomination or agitate against the Church to change her teachings. St. Mark Ji did not; he remained a steadfast Catholic despite being barred from the sacraments. He did not try to change the Church to conform to his behavior. He instead prayed for martyrdom. If you die for the Faith, your salvation is assured. Now, in Catholicism, martyrdom is when you are killed for being a Catholic. Being a Catholic was unpopular since it was regarded as a foreign religion; a Western colonial import.

In 1900, the Boxer Rebellion broke out. Its goals were the total expulsion of all Western influence from China. Christians were obvious targets.

Mark Ji and his family were arrested and in 1900, suffered beheading. Mark Ji's prayers were answered. He refused to renounce his Catholic Faith. He reportedly requested to be executed last, after his family, so he could encourage them and that none would die alone. This was granted. He was led to where he'd be executed, singing the Litany of the Blessed Virgin Mary the entire time, including up to when the blade separated his head from his body.

Countless other saints of various backgrounds can serve as inspiration for us in any situation, not just alcoholism and addictions. St. Margaret of Cortona was sexually promiscuous before her conversion. Likewise, St. Francis of Assisi was a "playboy" and party animal before his conversion. St. Bartolo Longo was a Satanist. Although she hasn't been canonized (yet), Dorothy Day had an abortion, had another child through a common-law marriage, and flirted with Marxism for a while before she found Truth in the Catholic Church and converted. She is a role model for orthodox Catholic social justice action.

When we feel depressed, or hopeless, are experiencing a case of terminal uniqueness, or are just afflicted with any situation, there is a saint (likely many) who has gone through the same thing. Don't assume just because someone lived 500 years ago or farther back in time, that they are no longer relevant and have nothing to offer. Time means nothing. Human nature is the same regardless of the culture or level of technology.

The mere practice of reading the lives of the saints may often be enough to lift one out of the emotional "place" you'd rather not be in. They make for great stories, often better than any fiction! Even though hagiographies (biographies of saints) from centuries past may seem overly pious or like embellished legends, there are essential truths in them about the basic facts of life. Perhaps some of the miraculous events didn't happen; then again, maybe they did. Were you there? Nevertheless, the process of reading a saint's life, regardless of the quality of the telling or the "unbelievable" tales, is edifying enough to help lift you out of the "where you're at" that you'd "rather not be."

XI: Get to know St. Joseph

One of the greatest saints of all (after the Blessed Virgin Mary, of course) is St. Joseph. The spouse of the Virgin Mary and foster-father of Jesus didn't leave behind any writings, and no words of his were ever recorded in Sacred Scripture. And yet the Church holds him up as the role model for men, families, laborers, and most especially for the Church herself as he is also Her Patron.

The Holy Trinity entrusted Joseph with the job of being the protector of the Blessed Virgin Mary and guardian of the Son of God, Jesus. Those are no small responsibilities. Joseph was to keep Mary safe and secure and provide for her, as well as serve as the father of the Messiah, the One Who was to redeem humankind.

You don't just pick anyone for the job. Therefore, Joseph is someone special. Given the tasks he was chosen to be responsible for, he must have been given tremendous graces and innate, natural skills to carry them out. Mother Angelica, the foundress of EWTN often said "God doesn't call the equipped, He equips the called." This is similar to the belief held by many saints of the past that God gives to those He has assigned a particular task the graces and natural gifts suited for that task. Given Joseph's role, God must have formed him through the power of divine grace to be the perfect protector of Mary and the foster father of Jesus.

Many of us have had issues with authority figures, whether Church or State or more local, such as our fathers. I am not going anywhere near trying to discuss the psychological issues attached to having a father. But given the importance of fatherhood:

how it was wielded in life, how your Dad treated you, and how you related to him is often at the core of many positive and negative attributes of life.

Many of us have a deep yearning for a good "father figure," a benign but gently strong leader with a moral compass aimed straight in the right direction. No father is perfect, (mine was all right, he had issues - who doesn't - but on the whole, I have no regrets over him being my Dad and I long to be reunited with him in Heaven), and some are much better than others. At times the expectations and needs of children may exceed the grasp of their father. At other times fathers have no clue what to do but they try their best. And some are downright awful. And all this contributes in varying degrees to our addictions.

While our fathers may have not been perfect, however many degrees of separation they each were from "the perfect father" that we all would have selected if given the choice, we do have someone who can serve as a kind of substitute, model, or guide. And that is St. Joseph.

How does this relate to the Sober Catholic Way? Even though there isn't a lot of quantifiable material in the Bible about him, that hasn't stopped a whole range of devotional cultures from developing around him. He is the patron saint of families, the Catholic men's spirituality movement, workers and hard laborers, migrants, those hoping for a "happy death" (i.e. to die in a state of grace), and numerous other things. (There is a devotional practice called the "Nine First Wednesdays." Similar to the Nine First Fridays of Five First Saturdays, you attend Mass and receive Holy Communion for nine consecutive first Wednesdays of the month and petition St. Joseph to die a happy death; as in, for whenever it happens!) You can explore the culture surrounding St. Joseph and adopt and adapt to your own needs. The fact that he is so close to Jesus and Mary and had authority over them, and must have been selected for the role he lived out makes him a mighty intercessor.

Research Catholic books and sites on St. Joseph and see how well he can supply for whatever was lacking in your own father or how well he can aid your parenthood. There's a bibliography in Appendix G: "Resources on Recovery" to help get you started. St. Joseph can serve as a model for you in many ways.

XII: Live the Beatitudes

I had read somewhere that the "Beatitudes," (part of the "Sermon on the Mount") are referred to as the "Be-attitudes," as they reflect a "proper attitude of being." In studying the Beatitudes and learning what they mean, you learn the right attitude toward living, and with this orientation, develop a blessed way of living. We are blessed and in a state of grace in our relationship with God.

Matthew 5:1-12:
"When Jesus saw the crowds, he went up the mountain,
and after he had sat down, his disciples came to him.
He began to teach them, saying:
'Blessed are the poor in spirit,
for theirs is the Kingdom of heaven.
Blessed are they who mourn,
for they will be comforted.
Blessed are the meek,
for they will inherit the land.
Blessed are they who hunger and thirst for
righteousness,
for they will be satisfied.
Blessed are the merciful,
for they will be shown mercy.
Blessed are the clean of heart,
for they will see God.
Blessed are the peacemakers,

for they will be called children of God.
Blessed are they who are persecuted for the sake of
righteousness,
for theirs is the Kingdom of heaven.
Blessed are you when they insult you and persecute you
and utter every kind of evil against you falsely because
of me.
Rejoice and be glad,
for your reward will be great in heaven.
Thus they persecuted the prophets who were before
you.'"

By a "proper attitude of being," I mean attitudes and
actions that are formed and guided by Catholic moral and social
teachings, of which the Catechism of the Church, and Sacred
Scripture, are the sources for these.

Let's take a look at the Beatitudes:

Blessed are the poor in spirit,
for theirs is the Kingdom of heaven.

Poor in spirit is "humility." Humility is accepting
ourselves for who we are not who we think we are; accepting reality
for what it is, adjusting your life to fit that reality, and being content
with the results.

How can we practice humility? Putting others before yourself. Considering the needs of others before your own needs; this is almost a "must" if you are a part of a family, but it can be also applied to your neighborhood or workplace. Chapters 13 through 18 also offer numerous examples and suggestions.

> *Blessed are they who mourn,*
>> *for they will be comforted.*

Mourning could mean missing those in our lives who have died. It could also mean sorrow for our sins, for they can cause the death of the Divine life in our souls.

How can we practice this? With the former, grieving properly and praying for the dead are helpful. Develop a devotion to the Holy Souls in Purgatory. For the latter, since it involves "sorrow for sins," perhaps working out the Devotions to the Sacred and Immaculate Hearts of Mary, and offering up reparative and redemptive suffering for your sins and those of others.

> *Blessed are the meek,*
>> *for they will inherit the land.*

To be meek, or to have meekness, is to have self-control and self-discipline. All of us former practicing alcoholics and addicts can use a huge dose of meekness. Meekness can also impact our lives in numerous other ways, including improving our interpersonal relationships.

How can we practice this? (Like I'm the one to advise on self-control and self-discipline.) It looks like "practicing humility" will contribute to these traits; in humbling yourself you must exert a great degree of self-control and self-discipline. You can also practice some of the lessons learned in the rooms of Twelve Step movements, such as remembering your last drunk. Do you want to return to that? An increase in your self-control and self-discipline will have a remarkable impact on your sobriety, as well as improve the state of your soul.

> *Blessed are they who hunger and thirst for righteous-*
> *ness,*
> > *for they will be satisfied.*

Think society lacks justice and righteousness? You are not alone. Practice the Corporal and Spiritual Works of Mercy (See Appendix D) to help move society along the path to a just society.

> *Blessed are the merciful,*
> > *for they will be shown mercy.*

Remember the final petitions of the Lord's Prayer. "Forgive us our trespasses as we forgive those who trespass against us." Do you want God to forgive your sins? You must be merciful and forgive others. For more ideas, please see Chapter 14: "Live the Divine Mercy Message."

> *Blessed are the clean of heart,*
> *for they will see God.*

Your focus is God. You have no strange Gods before Him. You are clean and sober and have put God first, before all others. Your heart beats for God. This doesn't mean you've forsaken marriage and relationships and gone off to be a hermit in the desert or a cave, but everyone knows that God is first in your life and they're OK with that.

> *Blessed are the peacemakers,*
> *for they will be called children of God.*

Pretty much what that says. You make peace. You are peaceful. You eschew violence. You build bridges between people. You are a uniter, not a divider.

Blessed are they who are persecuted for the sake of righteousness, for theirs is the Kingdom of heaven.

Blessed are you when they insult you and persecute you and utter every kind of evil against you falsely because of me.

Rejoice and be glad, for your reward will be great in heaven.

Thus they persecuted the prophets who were before you.

It's not easy being a Catholic or any kind of Christian. I've seen online news that states Christianity is the world's most persecuted religion. And in the United States and elsewhere, it's been said that anti-Catholicism is the last acceptable form of bigotry.

So, is this all-comprehensive lifestyle change aspect of the Sober Catholic Way easy? No, nothing worthwhile is. But we are to at least try. Attempting to live out the Beatitudes will help reform our lives and improve our ability to remove the character defects from our lives. Jesus rewards our efforts.

XIII: Live the Little Way of St. Therese

St. Therese of the Child Jesus and Holy Face, better known as "The Little Flower" or St. Therese of Lisieux, is one of the most popular saints within the Catholic Church. Canonized in 1925 only 28 years after her death from tuberculosis at the age of 24, she has captivated millions through her autobiography, "The Story of a Soul." It details her life from childhood through entering the cloistered Carmel monastery in Lisieux, France, with a rich exposition of her love for Jesus and His Mother. Throughout the book, the reader learns of her spirituality: that being the love (of the sacrificial and redemptive kind) and mercy of God. It was an antidote to the pharisaical and Jansenist Catholicism that dominated 19th-century France and it remains a strong counterforce to similar attitudes amongst Catholics of today.

One of the most influential aspects of "The Story of a Soul" lies in its explanation of the Little Flower's doctrine of "The Little Way." Commonly understood, her Little Way is the application of the Gospel to everyday situations. You do everything with love and humility. You seek and find God and His will in the ordinary.

Jesus did not seek greatness. He was a poor, itinerant preacher who associated with the lowest dregs of society: hookers, drunks, lepers, the poor, the outcast, and government officials. To quote St. Paul in his Letter to the Philippians 2:6:

For this understanding in you was also in Christ Jesus:
who, though he was in the form of God, did not consider
equality with God something to be seized. Instead, he
emptied himself, taking the form of a servant, being made
in the likeness of men, and accepting the state of a man.
He humbled himself, becoming obedient even unto death,
even death on the Cross.

And that is a key part of understanding how the Little Way
is the Applied Gospel for Ordinary Folk.

Jesus did not exalt His divinity; He never used it as an
excuse to avoid "being little," for He always humbled Himself in
service to His people.

And this was from the beginning of His Earthly life; for
He descended to Earth not as a fully grown human male or as a
mighty warrior-king or firebrand prophet. No, God became Little, a
humble, innocent baby, subject to and dependent upon His human
parents.

God defined and established the Little Way by the very act
of His Incarnation; nearly 1,900 years later He raised up St. Therese
to bring that fact to life in modern times in a new way that applies to
all.

The Little Way is described as the quickest and easiest
path to Salvation. St. Therese taught that by doing ordinary things
with great care and especially with love, you will win the heart of
Jesus and He will bear witness to you before the Father when you
appear for your Judgment.

We quite often look at the "little things" of life as
annoying stuff we have to put up with. St. Therese saw them as the

pathway to Heaven. Each "little thing," be it picking up something that fell to the floor, sweeping up that floor, raking the leaves, or not complaining when someone is being difficult; all of these things are acts of love to one's neighbor.

People idolize the so-called "elites" of society: those who do things that bring them glory, honor, and fame. For most politicians, athletes, and celebrities, the little things are beneath them. And so they are beneath those who regard them as role models. The Little Way of St. Therese turns this upside down. It is the Gospel expression of the Beatitudes (See Chapter 12), of answering Jesus' call to take up His Cross and follow Him, or rejecting what the World thinks of as important.

It is being "little," and not "big." It is living a humble life as opposed to a life where you seek power, control, and domination over others. It's a life where you do not make demands. Instead, it is a life where you seek to offer help to others and to make appeals to their better nature. Political activists and social justice advocates should take notice that it is often far better to make gentle appeals to people than make strident demands on them.

The Little Way is an essential part of living the Sober Catholic Way. Matt Talbot lived the Little Way (See Chapter 18: "Live the Matt Talbot Way.") You can see the Little Way in the Serenity Prayer that Twelve Steppers memorize to get them through difficult moments.

The keys to understanding the Little Way are love and humility. True love implies self-sacrifice. You give of yourself for the other without regard to the cost to yourself. Humility (or

Littleness) is accepting yourself as you are, in the role God planned for you.

God was Little; and as John the Evangelist tells us, "For God is love." (1 John 4:8)

God's Littleness was expressed in His Incarnation; and His Love in the Passion, Death, and Resurrection of Christ Jesus.

Therefore, the Little Way replicates the Incarnation using our becoming "Little" like Jesus did when He entered Mary's womb, and the act of doing "little things" such as our daily tasks and duties with great love requires us to sacrifice our self-will and self-love. This, in turn, replicates the Passion, Death, and Resurrection of Jesus.

The Little Way therefore combines in our daily lives the mission of Our Lord in His Incarnation and Passion.

So, finite, limited creatures like us can be Christ-bearers to others simply by living out our daily existence in humility. Just doing our little daily tasks with love and humility. Not ever thinking greatly of ourselves, no self-importance. Just by being Little.

From simplicity comes such great things. Who can tell what impact some "little" thing you do might have on someone? Someone may be having a bad day until you did some nice little thing for them; maybe you just smiled, but it changed them for the better.

"The Story of a Soul" wasn't only about the Little Way. It also revealed St. Therese's prayer life and pious acts. (By "pious," I am referring to an older use of the word, that of a loving duty to God.)

She had a zeal in receiving the Eucharist. I don't remember at all the day I received First Holy Communion, nor the time preparing for it. For St. Therese, it was one of the singularly important events in her childhood. She understood and knew that she was receiving her Saviour, all Body, Blood, Soul, and Divinity of Him. If you ever get to feeling blasé about receiving Our Lord in the Eucharist, study her writings on her First Holy Communion.

Next to receiving the Eucharist, her devotion to adoring Jesus in the Blessed Sacrament was profound. She found great solace in her solitude with Him. (See Chapter 2)

She had great zeal for studying the catechism. The catechism in her day was the "Roman Catechism" also known as the "Catechism of the Council of Trent." Perhaps she also had a children's adaptation, but I wouldn't be surprised if she read the primary catechism, at least after entering the cloister.

She also studied Sacred Scripture, especially the Letters of St. Paul (where she discovered her vocation.) Get a good Catholic Bible; non-Catholic ones leave out several books and even the "good" non-Catholic Bibles might have doctrinal explanations that are not in agreement with the Catholic Church; or they just ignore explaining something. You are Catholic; there is no excuse to use a non-Catholic Bible. At all! (See Chapter 3)

She also read the classic medieval book, "The Imitation of Christ" by Thomas a Kempis. It was very important to her, so much so that she had it memorized. Stories are told in which her family would play a game: they would mention a Book, Chapter, and Paragraph number to her, and Therese would correctly recite that selection. A pocket version of it was her constant companion. (See Chapter 5)

She devoured books on the lives of the saints, especially her heroine, St. Joan of Arc. These helped form her faith. Any saint will do; we are all attracted to different ones. The Holy Spirit will lead you to some. They may even pick you! Those that others are attracted to may not inspire you. We are all unique, as are the saints. And like in real life, everyone is attracted to different people. (See Chapter 10.)

She found great solace also in communication through prayer with residents of her Heavenly Homeland. Not just St. Joan of Arc and other saints she was attracted to, but also her mother, who died while Therese was a child, as well as her deceased siblings, (her parents had several children who died in infancy. She received signal graces from them all, signs her prayers were heard. Heaven was real to her, a destination that life on Earth was just a means to get to. It was not some hopeful fantasy. (Although she was stricken with doubts about it near the end of her life.)

One book she read that meant a lot to her was "The End of the Present World and the Mysteries of the Future Life," by Father Charles Arminjon. A series of conferences or seminars given by that priest in France in 1881, the subject matter of death and salvation inspired a transformation in St. Therese, who said it "plunged my soul into a state of joy, not of this earth." Shortly afterwards she began her attempts to enter the cloister of Carmel in Lisieux.

Along with all of the above, the autobiography is priceless in terms of her teachings on the value of suffering, poverty, and humility, all of which are wrapped up in her Little Way.

St. Therese of Lisieux is a saint for all of us. She is "little," not impressed with the importance of secular things; she is yet another little person that God selected to shame the proud. Her Little Way is the antidote crucially needed for civilization in these times of pride, identity, and insanity. But for Catholics seeking a way to holiness and a sure path to God and Heaven, the Little Way of St. Therese is the means to our ultimate destiny. By it, we can all become great saints. It is also a way for us to cope with the situations afflicting the Church (any of them).

Make her your own. She loves everyone, even you, regardless of what you think of yourself. More importantly, regardless of what others think of you. She will lead you to God and help you become a saint. It is not an impossible task and she shows the way. God is Love, Jesus came to do the Will of His Father, and the Little Way is how each of us can achieve that in our daily activities.

How is this all connected to the Sober Catholic Way? You may notice that many of the points made in this chapter also are chapters in themselves. That's the importance of St. Therese in maintaining sobriety. Matt Talbot (See Chapter 18: "Live the Matt Talbot Way") was a devotee of St. Therese. In fact, "To Slake A Thirst: The Matt Talbot Way to Sobriety," by Philip Maynard, calls her the "Theologian of the Matt Talbot Way."

XIV: Live the Divine Mercy Message

Living the Divine Mercy Message is to place your confidence in Jesus' Mercy and to live a life where Mercy towards others and yourself is the cornerstone.

"Jesus, I Trust in You" is the signature phrase or prayer of the Divine Mercy Message. It is unconditional and all-encompassing. Your faith in Jesus is the rock that helps you to endure those difficult times when you may despair or become despondent.

St. Faustina Kowalska was a Polish nun who had received messages (or "interior locutions") from Jesus and the Blessed Virgin Mary for several years before she died in 1938. Jesus commanded her to write her experiences. The resulting book, "Divine Mercy in My Soul," is a modern-day classic of Catholic spirituality and mysticism. As with all Church-approved apparitions and locutions, there is nothing in her Diary that adds anything "new" to divine revelation. These are an accepted part of Catholicism but are not binding upon the faithful. Apparitions like those at Guadalupe, Lourdes, and Fatima and messages such as those received by Sr. Faustina (now Saint Faustina) are merely signs that the Good Shepherd is doing His work and is reminding us of certain things we seem to have forgotten. Quite often apparitions and locutions occur during critical moments in human history, indicating that the Lord's "sheep" are going astray and He is coming after them. They exhort us to do things we already should be doing but most have strayed from.

Jesus' messages to St. Faustina concern God's immense love for people and His boundless "Ocean of Mercy" to which we are all entitled. No matter how dirty we have become by the sins of our past when we dip into the ocean of Mercy, we are scrubbed clean. God's mercy is available to us for the asking and is the source of immeasurable graces.

The devotion and practice of Divine Mercy is critical, I think, to anyone in recovery. It fixes our brokenness and mends our wounded souls. It teaches us that God is a loving Father, that Jesus is our brother, and the Holy Spirit is our infallible guide.

It was important to me and critical in my recovery and how my Catholic Faith became more important than the Twelve Steps in maintaining my sobriety.

The key elements of the Divine Mercy Devotion are:

+The diary of St. Faustina ("Divine Mercy in My Soul.")
+The Image of Divine Mercy
+The Chaplet of Divine Mercy
+The Divine Mercy Novena
+The Hour of Mercy
+Divine Mercy Sunday

"Divine Mercy in My Soul" is a spiritual autobiography detailing her life from her youth through to just before her death, a wonderful description of a life lived according to the Will of God. Unlike most autobiographies, the chronology is a little off because she was duped into burning an early draft of it and when told by her confessor to write it all again, she wrote her recollections of the destroyed parts alongside the new material. However, this is no obstacle to understanding and appreciating the book: reading it is like diving into a pool of grace-filled baptismal waters and swimming about and soaking up the wellsprings of mercy. You emerge changed and convinced that despite how unworthy you are, God loves you and wants you with Him forever in Heaven and His Mercy is the key to that journey.

The Image of Mercy is the painting commissioned by St. Faustina from instructions given to her by Jesus. He requested that a painting be made of what she saw during an apparition. The Merciful Jesus image (there are several versions) depicts Jesus with an arm raised in a blessing with rays of light beaming outward from His heart. One ray is red which symbolizes His Precious Blood (the life-giving sacrament of the Eucharist) and the other is white (the waters of Baptism.)

The Image of the Merciful Jesus is available anywhere Catholic devotional items are sold and is even found nowadays in most churches. Get one for yourself; Jesus said that anyone who venerates it, especially during the Hour of Mercy, receives a plenitude of graces including those for final perseverance. It's also pretty.

The Chaplet of Divine Mercy is a devotion using ordinary rosary beads. It is too long to go into here (see the resources in Appendix G) but it is a prayer taught to St. Faustina by Jesus that devotees are to say every day, especially during the Hour of Mercy. It contains petitions for mercy for the petitioner and the whole world. In praying it, you are acting as an intercessor for the human race.

The Divine Mercy Novena is said annually from Good Friday until the Saturday before the Second Sunday of Easter (what used to be known as Low Sunday,) which is now Divine Mercy Sunday. Jesus requested that the Novena be recited during this period (although you can say it at other times during the year.) Every day the object of the petition changes; again, it's too long to go into here: wherever you obtain your Image of the Merciful Jesus, you can probably get instructions on how to pray it.

The Hour of Mercy is at 3 PM local time. It is the Hour when Jesus died on the Cross and when the floodgates of mercy opened up from His Sacred Side when the lance pierced it. Every day the Divine Mercy devotees pray the Chaplet during this hour, if they cannot due to work or other obstacles, they recite (hopefully right at 3 O'clock, otherwise anytime during the hour) this prayer:

"O Blood and Water which gushed forth from the side of
Jesus as a fountain of mercy for us, have Mercy on us and
on the whole world."

Divine Mercy Sunday is the feast day for the Divine Mercy Devotion. There are plenary indulgences attached to going to Mass on that day. Unlike the typical requirement for plenary indulgences that you cannot have any attachment to sin, on this day that is set aside. The floodgates of mercy open up upon all those who participate in the festivities. I love this holyday, I look forward to it every year. Celebrating it was instrumental in my reversion to the Church after years of being away.

Jesus gave us instructions as to how to live the Divine Mercy Message. There is a threefold level of progression based on ability and opportunity. Listed in paragraph 742 of the Diary, Jesus said that the first is performing deeds of mercy towards our neighbor. It should be obvious what these are, but the Corporal and Spiritual Works of Mercy are a good start (see Appendix D) as well as working out the Little Way of St. Therese (see Chapter 13.) If you cannot do those, you can perform a work of mercy by saying words of mercy. The final way is through prayers for mercy. Everyone can pray and if you're reading this you probably do or are learning to and starting.

How is this related to the Sober Catholic Way? Living the Divine Mercy Message of deeds, words, and prayers of mercy links all of the basic elements of Catholic spirituality, especially when including the Little Way of St. Therese and the Matt Talbot Way (see Chapter 18) and the Gospel.

This is important to all of us Catholic alcoholics and addicts. We are so broken and wounded from our past. For many, the past is just too much and they never fully escape from being haunted by it.

The all-encompassing nature of Divine Mercy heals our souls and enables us to draw upon the endless reservoir of God's Mercy. It is a tremendous aid in our spiritual growth and progress. It led me back into the Catholic Church, with Her fullness of the Gospel Truth and the sacramental life and graces. It helps you to achieve a fuller life.

XV: Live the Message of Guadalupe

Living the Message of Guadalupe is to live a life respecting others and valuing their dignity as persons. It embraces other people despite cultural and racial differences and cherishes all life, from natural conception to natural death. Quite simply, we put a Catholic twist on the multiculturalism, tolerance, pro-abortion, assisted suicide, affirmative action, diversity, equity, and inclusion agendas of today, as well as being open to seeing other Christians as members of the Mystical Body of Christ. This is the radical proposition St. Paul the Apostle wrote about in his First Letter to the Corinthian (1 Cor 12:12-31) where he said in verses 12-14:

> For just as the body is one, and yet has many parts, so all the parts of the body, though they are many, are only one body. So also is Christ.

> And indeed, in one Spirit, we were all baptized into one body, whether Jews or Gentiles, whether servant or free. And we all drank in the one Spirit.

> For the body, too, is not one part, but many.

How is this related to the Guadalupe Message?

When Our Lady appeared to Juan Diego over several days in early December of 1531, Mexico was going through some very trying times. The Spanish had arrived in 1519. Over the next two years, they conquered the Aztecs with the assistance of numerous other indigenous nations who were only too happy to lend their numerical strength to the Spaniards' advanced military technology and end forever the Aztec's constant warring against them to feed their need for human sacrifices. For you see, the Aztecs had adapted their religion over the previous several decades to add human sacrifice to their ritual observances. This was not popular with the other nations or even many Aztecs.

The Spaniards put an immediate stop to this practice when they achieved control.

However, abuses arose over the next decade: the Spanish colonial government abused and exploited the Mexicans and resisted all attempts by the Catholic Church to stop them. It wasn't until the Bishop of Mexico City managed to smuggle out a message to Spain that the Spanish King effected the appropriate reforms. There were still problems, however. Abuses still occurred, but the Church had to authority to deal with that. But the preeminent issue was that the Aztecs had endured a massive cultural paradigm shift: from being an imperialistic conquering nation to becoming a subjugated one, with their pagan religious practices suppressed. Their moral compass wasn't pointing anywhere in particular.

They were on the brink of rebellion.

Enter Our Lady. At a crucial time, Our Lady did her motherly thing and appeared to a Christian indigenous man and gave him a message of peace and love. Her appearance was heavy with symbolism significant to both the Aztecs and the Spanish.

It is beyond the scope of this book to detail the story of the apparition, see Appendix G for good books to read. But in short, (and I don't do it justice) from December 9 – 12, 1531, Our Lady appeared to an indigenous man by the name of Juan Diego. He heard mysterious music while passing by Tepeyac Hill, just outside Mexico City. He made his way to its top where he encountered beautiful flowers and bird songs. He thought he had entered the paradisical realm his ancient Aztec ancestors had believed in. Our Lady appeared and informed him who she was (the Mother of the One True God) and that she wanted him to see the Bishop and have a little chapel built where they were. This was difficult as there were ethnic and class distinctions that typically prohibited such meetings. The meetings with the Bishop were indeed fruitless. The Bishop eventually demanded a sign as proof of who was speaking to Juan. The proof was given in the form of beautiful Castilian roses that suddenly appeared growing on the barren, rocky hilltop, and out-of-season no less! Juan Diego was instructed by Our Lady to retrieve them in his tilma (a work apron) and bring them to her. She rearranged them and told him to take them to the Bishop. He did, and when he opened the tilma, the roses tumbled out to the astonishment of the Bishop and his aides, and an image of Our Lady formed right before them on the tilma. The image was not just of Our Lady. She was wearing clothing with designs on it that were of tremendous significance to both the Aztecs and the Spanish. The image lasts to this day, nearly 500 years later. The tilma would normally have disintegrated within a few decades, but its condition is the same as it was in 1531. As with regards to the image, it has been studied by rigorous scientific means, and no known human methods of painting it can be discerned. Furthermore, the eyes of Our Lady in the image were examined and they reflect an image of the scene in the Bishop's office when the tilma was opened! There is no known way to do this, especially in the 16th Century. She is also depicted as being pregnant, hence she is a patronness of the Pro-Life movement. Given the Aztecs previous practice of human sacrifice, this signifies the sacredness of all life, from womb to tomb. She is also associated with the largest voluntary mass conversion of people to Catholicism. Fourteen years after the Protestant Revolt in Europe which stripped millions from the One True Faith, millions of pagans in Mexico replaced them through her intercession! How's that for racial equality?! Millions of people of color became Catholics and replaced millions of white Europeans who left the Church!

There is an ever-increasing list of miraculous or otherwise unexplainable phenomena associated with the tilma. I say "ever-increasing list" because although the phenomena dates to 1531, some weren't detectable until more modern technology became available to researchers. Again, see Appendix G for books that have this information.

The essential Message of Guadalupe as related by Our Lady's words and the designs on the tilma is one of mutual cultural respect. It encourages or blesses the fusion of cultures across the racial and ethnic divides. We are to see each other as unique individuals with equal dignity, made in the image and likeness of God. As baptized Christians, we are members of the Mystical Body of Christ first and see others as members or potential members of that Mystical Body. Any other identity, such as race (White, Black, and so on,) ethnicity (American, Mexican, European, Chinese, etc.), and political affiliation (liberal or conservative,) follows. We should always view each other in that context.

Why is this a part of the Sober Catholic Way? We must always seek to "be the change we wish to see" in others and society. In AA, things unrelated to personal recovery are considered "outside issues" and are irrelevant to Twelve Step recovery (and for good reason, recovery programs *should* just focus on keeping people clean and sober. Expanding into non-recovery issues just invites division and controversy.) Catholics are called to evangelize according to whatever their state in life is. We are to be the Book of the Gospels that others see.

We are to be the leaven of society, the yeast that makes the bread rise, and be the loaf it was made to be.

So, again, "Why is this a part of the Sober Catholic Way?" How does this message of non-divisive cultural fusion and respect keep us sober?

The Message of Guadalupe, when it is internalized (made a part of our inner self, our soul) helps us to see other people as dignified individuals, regardless of race, ethnicity, and nationality. When we see others in this way, we achieve a type of internal peace. If we are at peace with ourselves, we can be at peace with others and we hardly need the drink or the drug.

Modern society tends to objectify people. It comes as no surprise that this objectification quickly becomes the basis for evaluating others. Everyone gets evaluated or identified by their race, gender, ideology, and so on. But when we see the humanity in others, we begin to see them as the persons they are and not as whatever their external identity is. We then also see the humanity in ourselves. To phrase it another way, when we do not objectify others according to their external identity, we do not objectify ourselves.

When this happens, we are less likely to turn to things that are harmful like alcohol, drugs, or pornography. All of these have as their root the objectification of the self. When you are objectified, whether by society or by yourself, you feel less human and less of a person. As a consequence, you are more likely to turn to an addictive substance in a futile attempt to regain your lost humanity or personhood.

So, live out the message of Guadalupe: you will reinforce your humanity and better reflect the image and likeness of God all the while seeing others as individual people, not objects that are representative examples of gender, race, or whatever other divisive category society invents. In this manner we not only heal and help ourselves, but society, too.

XVI: Live the Message of Lourdes

Living the Message of Lourdes is to live a life of prayer and penance. It is also to live a life where we turn to Our Lady (really, through Mary to Jesus) and pray for healing. The Apparition of Our Lady at Lourdes, France is a natural and obvious Marian Apparition for alcoholics and addicts to adopt as our "own." It is renowned for the over 7,000 inexplicable cures (so far only 70 have been recognized by the Church as truly miraculous) and countless spiritual healings.

How often had we prayed for a miraculous healing of our addiction?

Like the other apparitions mentioned in this book, it is beyond the scope to delve too deeply into the details, there are books in Appendix G on resources to read. But I'll briefly relate it here:

The Blessed Virgin Mary appeared to a 14-year-old girl named Bernadette Soubirous. She was poor, uneducated, and quite ignorant of the basics of Catholic doctrines. The first apparition occurred on February 11, 1858. The eighteenth and final took place on July 16th of that year.

She reported a mysterious vision in the grotto (a hollow) of the rock of Massabielle on the banks of the River Gave. It was that of a young and beautiful lady. But Bernadette was the only one who saw the vision, despite being accompanied by several other girls. During the later apparitions, many others from the town were present, hoping to see whatever Bernadette claimed to see, but no one ever did, save for Bernadette.

Bernadette often fell into ecstasy during the visits of Our Lady. At times Our Lady spoke to Bernadette who was also the only one who heard the voice. One day she was told to drink from a previously unknown fountain in the grotto. Bernadette dug where she was told and muddy water gushed forth. This is the fountain that was later discovered to possess miraculous healing properties. On another occasion, the apparition asked Bernadette to go and tell the priests she wished a chapel to be built on the spot and for processions (pilgrimages) to be made to the grotto. During the third apparition, she was requested to return 15 more times, although this was intentionally made difficult by her family and the Lourdes authorities. They all thought she was fabricating it. Until one day Bernadette, at the request of the town's priest, asked Our Lady who she was. Bernadette had until this point not known who the Lady was nor had ever referred to her as the Blessed Virgin. The Lady in the Apparition of March 25, 1858 (the Solemnity of the Annunciation) identified herself with the phrase, "I am the Immaculate Conception."

Now, the dogma of the Immaculate Conception had only been formally defined four years earlier, in 1854. Bernadette's education didn't include such matters. As was said before, based on her performance in class she was not considered to be a bright student. When she reported this self-identification to the priest he was astounded. There was no way the poor, seemingly stupid little student could have made that up. The doctrine is difficult to comprehend today, in the 21st Century. That was only more so in a rural, backwater village in the middle-of-nowhere France.

Bernadette's credibility soared.

The times Our Lady appeared in were becoming overrun with the ideas that rationalism, reason, logic, and science are the solutions to everything, and society had no room for antiquated superstitions like "God" and "religion."

But God intervenes in history through His Mama. Humankind can turn its back on Him and invent all sorts of nonsense to replace Him, but He never ignores us. The times of that 19th Century period were rapidly careening towards institutional atheism. Much like today, which we can only imagine how much worse it would be without the appearances and lessons of Our Lady back then.

How is the Apparition of Our Lady at Lourdes related to the Sober Catholic Way? We are sick people, regardless of the length of our sobriety. Our Lady of Lourdes is our special channel of healing graces. Jesus is the Divine Physician and He works through His Mother at Lourdes. Even if you cannot get to France, you can avail yourself through prayer and meditation of requests for spiritual healing. Adopt Our Lady of Lourdes and St. Bernadette Soubirous as your special patrons. Pope St. John Paul II had declared February 11th as the "World Day of the Sick," a special day for healing Masses and prayers for anyone suffering from any illness, malady, or disability. It's our feast day!

Furthermore, Our Lady told Bernadette several times about the need for penance. This strikes at the heart of who we are. For we have hurt and damaged others through the sins we committed against them during our active years of addiction. Penance is something we desperately need. It is one thing to use the Sacrament of Confession (which you should do at least once a month if you're serious about your spiritual growth and development.) We should also willingly "take up our Crosses" and accept those trials, troubles, and tribulations that come into our lives every day and offer them up in reparation for our sins and those of others.

There are other ways by which the Apparition of Our Lady of Lourdes belongs to the Sober Catholic Way. Just like Chapter 15: "Live the Message of Guadalupe" tells of the transformation of society (as a manifestation of our interior transformation which begets transformation in others) so does Lourdes.

It is more obvious to anyone who has been to Lourdes (I haven't, yet) or who has read accounts of those who had gone on pilgrimage there (I have!) But all report that there is a feeling of oneness with others. Everyone who is there is not whatever their "identity" is. All are sick pilgrims in need of healing.

There is also an additional dimension that I've read about. There is a feeling of being a part of the Universal Church, the Catholic Church, in all her global, international humanity. Races and nations are united. The truly important people are the sick, weak, troubled, and marginalized. The "little people;" not the cultural elites like athletes, celebrities, social media influencers, and billionaires.

"Living the Message of Lourdes" builds upon Guadalupe. Like in that chapter, the Message of Lourdes is unitive. It's not a divisive and destructive nationalism or racial superiority and cultural separatism. Taken together, Guadalupe and Lourdes insist upon the unity of humanity, the inherent dignity of ourselves, and the respect for ourselves and others that flows from this unity and dignity. And with that, comes sobriety.

We help build a culture where addictive substances aren't needed because it is a culture of love where individuals are valued for who they are as persons; they feel they are part of a community that cherishes and accepts them simply for who they are.

XVII: Live the Message of Fatima

Living the message of Fatima means a life living of prayer and reparation. Some specific acts accompany living out the Fatima Message, but first, let's get to the basics of what happened.

In 1917 the Blessed Virgin Mary appeared to three Portuguese shepherd children 6 times near the town of Aljustrel in the parish of Fatima. It is one of the best-known and documented Marian Apparitions. The first apparition took place on May 13, 1917.

Mary requested the children to pray a lot and to return to the site on the 13th of the month for the next 5 months. They did this until the last epic appearance in October.

The June Apparition occurred on the 13th, as Mary promised. Despite efforts at secrecy, word had gotten out that Mary was to appear and so the three little shepherd children were not alone; a small crowd was also present. Those gathered were praying the Rosary.

Mary appeared but was only visible to the children. Mary reiterated what she had requested during the May 13th Apparition, that the shepherds were to return on the 13th of each month through October and pray much as well as learn to read.

She also confirmed another thing that she had said in May: two of the children will be going home to Heaven shortly (St. Francisco Marto and his sister St. Jacinta Marto.)

Mary also stated that the Lord wishes that there shall be a devotion to the Immaculate Heart of Mary.

On July 13, 1917, Our Lady appeared to the seers of Fatima for the third time. This was one of the most memorable and crucial of the six, perhaps second only to the last one on October 13 with its Miracle of the Sun.

For on this day, the three seers were gifted with a vision of Hell.

The children saw people falling into Hell and the indescribable torments they suffered from demons. Some of the demons appeared to be animals of unknown species. (Few ever bring that part up but it's always intrigued me. It's probably because I consumed mass quantities of science-fiction when I was young.)

The children almost died from the fright and horror of what they saw. It affected them deeply and Sts. Jacinta and Francesco seemed particularly concerned with making reparations and offering sacrifices on behalf of people to prevent even more from falling into damnation.

> You saw hell where the souls of poor sinners go. To save them, God wishes to establish in the world devotion to my Immaculate Heart. If what I say to you is done, many souls will be saved and there will be peace. - The Blessed Virgin Mary, to the children.

There were three secrets imparted to the children by Our Lady. I'm not going to go into details of the second and third secrets, since the vision of Hell was the first of the "Three Secrets of Fatima" and the secrets are beyond the scope of this book. See the resources in Appendix G.

The Fatima Apparition of August 13, 1917, did not occur when it was supposed to. The three seers of Fatima: Lucia, Jacinta, and Francisco had been taken "hostage" by the local government administrator just before the Apparition. As a result, they were not present but were miles away being threatened with torture (being boiled in oil) if they did not reveal the "Secret" that the Blessed Virgin Mary had shared with them earlier (the vision of Hell, amongst other things).

Nevertheless, Mary was not about to be upstaged or thwarted by a mere bureaucrat. Our Lady did appear later to the shepherd children on August 19th.

During this Apparition, our Lady requested that the seers continue to return on the 13th of the month and to continue praying the Rosary.

Lucia asked her as to what they should do with the money that was beginning to be donated. Mary replied that two "litters" (like stretchers to carry someone) are to be made, one to be carried by Lucia, Jacinta, and some girls, the other by Francisco and some boys, for the Feast of Our Lady of the Rosary. Money left over is to be used for the construction of a chapel to be built on the site.

Mary concluded with:

Pray, pray a lot, and offer sacrifices for the sinners. You
know that many souls go the hell because there is none
who pray for them.

By the time of the fifth Apparition in September, the popularity (or notoriety) of the event was growing. On the 13th of September, 30,000 people had gathered in the Cova de Iria to witness whatever was going to happen. The secular, anti-clerical atheistic press ramped up their ridicule.

After the usual questions posed to Mary about what she wanted, the seers were exhorted to continue to pray the Rosary. Otherwise, it seemed that all that happened was the seers asked questions about certain individuals and whether intercessions for them would be answered. (Some will, some won't. An important consideration to be aware of when you pray is never to assume your prayer will be answered in the manner you wish.)

After a final reminder to return for the final apparition on October 13th, Mary disappeared back to Heaven.

On October 13, 1917, the final Marian Apparition took place.

Seventy thousand people attended the event which was supposed to have a miracle promised by the Virgin Mary so that all may believe.

Amongst those present were representatives of the Portuguese media, all socialist and all anti-clerical (theophobes who despised the Catholic Church, professed atheism, and cooperated in what they hoped would be the eventual destruction of the Church in Portugal. The country had undergone a revolution in 1910 which deposed the Catholic monarchy and imposed restrictions on the Church.)

Our Lady appeared as promised, but she was not alone. St. Joseph also appeared and was holding the Christ Child.

The sun also danced in the sky. Witnessed by the 70,000 in attendance and by others hundreds of miles away, the sun whirled about in the sky, emitting multicolor beams of light that terrified the witnesses.

It also appeared to hurtle towards the Earth which convinced people that the World was ending.

One note on the sun dancing: for anyone who may be skeptical, evidence that it happened lies in the fact that it had been raining heavily all day long, so much so that the ground throughout the area was drenched. Saturated with water, and combined with the foot traffic of 70,000 attendees, it was a horrific muddy mess.

Until the sun dried it almost instantly. According to all those present, after the Apparition was over and the sun returned to its normal state, the ground was hardened as if it had not rained for weeks.

And another note for skeptics: this was all duly reported by the anti-clerical, socialist media. The reporters had gone there hoping (more likely assuming) that the whole event would be a non-happening; that the seers would be shamed, the Church embarrassed, and once and for all the foolish believers would have their religious superstitions exposed for what they are – utter nonsense.

But no, they couldn't deny the event, their skepticism and non-belief didn't prevent them from witnessing the Miracle of the Sun and reporting it, along with acknowledging its effects on the physical environment.

So much for that. How the whole thing happened is a mystery. How only those in the vicinity witnessed this, but for people all over the rest of the world the Sun operated normally is known only to God, who is not subject to the laws of Nature. (That's why certain events are called "miracles." Perhaps someday, when science progresses to a more sophisticated level, someone can postulate a theory explaining localized solar phenomena. But until science catches up with Faith...)

During a follow-up Apparition to Lucia in 1925, The "Five First Saturdays" were instituted at the request of Mary. Although I mentioned these in Chapter 6, they bear repeating:

On the first Saturday of the month for five consecutive months, the faithful should:

+Go to Confession

+Receive Holy Communion

+pray the Rosary

+meditate on one of the mysteries for fifteen minutes

+all of the above in a spirit of reparation

+Confession can be eight days before or after the Saturday.

+Communion can be received in the usual ways: either at Mass, such as a Saturday morning daily Mass or the Saturday Evening Vigil Mass, or from a priest or Eucharistic Minister, or during a Communion Service. Many parishes may have such a service to assist people in fulfilling their requirements. Check around your locale at Mass Times for parishes.

Why five Saturdays? To atone for the five ways in which people offend the Immaculate Heart of Mary:

+attacks upon Mary's Immaculate Conception

+attacks upon her perpetual virginity

+attacks upon her Divine Maternity and the refusal to accept her as the Mother of all mankind

+for those who try to publicly implant in children's hearts indifference, contempt, and even hatred of this Immaculate Mother

+for those who insult her directly in her sacred images.

How does living the Fatima Message belong to the Sober Catholic Way? "Prayer, Conversion and Penance." These are the core strategies for those of us struggling with alcoholism. It is the Sober Catholic Way. We pray, we have an ongoing conversion, and we live penitential lives. Or, we do this as best we can. Some times and years are better than others. But we trudge on. This is not just for ourselves; Our Lady indicates that we were to also pray for others, particularly those who do not pray and who live sinful lives.

Fatima may also be that apparition that steps in when we do not learn and apply the messages of Guadalupe and Lourdes. Where they call upon the unity and dignity of people and their culture, and suggest a blending of them as a sign of our unity in the Mystical Body of Christ, Fatima is there when all that fails. When the Messages of Guadalupe and Lourdes aren't heeded, there is strife, hatred, and sin. Then a different Message must be heard.

XVIII: Live the Matt Talbot Way

Matt Talbot was an Irish hard laborer and ex-drunk who, if he ever gets around to miraculously interceding for a couple of people, will be beatified and then canonized. Afterward, he will become the patron saint of alcoholics and laborers. June 19th is his feast day.

Since you have this book you probably know of him; how he was a drunk, begging and borrowing money to support his pub crawling, lending money when he had it to support others' drinking habits, and how on that awful day when he had no money, and worse, no beer, turned out he also had no "real" friends either. It was that awful day when no one wanted to spot him any more cash and Matt discovered he had no access to the drink. On that awful day he decided to "take the pledge;" the total abstinence from the drink.

It worked, and Matt led a life of humble piety, going to daily Mass, reciting the Rosary every day, and reading many spiritual books, including "Total Consecration to the Blessed Virgin Mary," by St. Louis deMontfort.

Matt had a strong devotion to the Sacred Heart. Matt's prayer life and means of staying sober involved transferring his "love for the drink" onto the Sacred Heart of Jesus. In essence, you give your addiction to Him. If you pick up the bottle or whatever your addiction is again, you are taking back your gift from Jesus.

He took to heart the admonition to "seek first the kingdom," and made a throne for the Sacred Heart in his soul.

"Where your heart is, there shall your treasure be," and the treasure of Matt's heart was Jesus' Sacred Heart and His Most Immaculate Mother, Mary.

It is said that Matt's piety, devotion, and sacramental life led him to live out the Twelve Steps of Alcoholics Anonymous decades before they were ever conceived. He essentially discovered them independently of Bill Wilson (AA's Founder.) He understood that he was powerless over the drink that had made a mess of his life, decided to turn his life over to God, made frequent examinations of his conscience and went to Confession, made amends and built a life a prayer and Catholic action. This should silence all Catholic critics of AA and the Steps who claim it fosters indifferentism. It does, if one's Faith is weak, but if you simultaneously reach out and explore the spiritual riches of your Catholic Faith while also working the Steps, just like Matt did, you should become a stronger Catholic.

How does this belong to the Sober Catholic Way? The Matt Talbot Way to Sobriety encompasses virtually every single thing in this book, I just added my personal experiences and flourishes. Matt did it all, except for things occurring long after he died, such as the Divine Mercy Devotion and probably Fatima. (News of Fatima most likely didn't become well-known in Ireland until long after his death in 1925.) But chances are good he would have done everything I suggest in this book.

You can summarize the Matt Talbot Way in this manner:

+Every day after awakening make your Daily Morning Offering. This is the traditional one, but any will do that unites your intentions to Jesus and Mary and includes offering up your suffering:

> O Jesus, through the Immaculate Heart of Mary, I offer you my prayers, works, joys, and sufferings of this day for all the intentions of your Sacred Heart in union with the Holy Sacrifice of the Mass throughout the world, for the salvation of souls, the reparation of sins, the reunion of all Christians, and in particular for the intentions of the Holy Father this month. Amen

+Any other prayers dedicated to Jesus and His Blessed Mother.

+Invocations to the Holy Spirit. There are numerous prayers to the Holy Spirit, pick one that suits you or make up your own.

+Spiritual reading. Matt was not alone in immersing himself in reading the Lives of the Saints or the writings they left behind. The spiritual reading needn't be the writings of saints, there are classic and contemporary writings of great worth by solidly orthodox Catholics.

+Frequent recollection throughout the day. Even Twelve Step movements recommend this, only they call it "Step 10." A part of your recollection should be prayer, perhaps the Fatima Sacrifice prayer:

> Oh, my Jesus, it is for love of Thee, in reparation for the offenses committed against the Immaculate Heart of Mary, and for the conversion of poor sinners. Amen.

+Or the Divine Mercy 3 o'clock Prayer (whether or not it's 3 PM. To paraphrase a popular song from a few decades ago, "It's 3 o'clock Somewhere":

> "O Blood and Water which gushed forth from the side of Jesus as a fountain of mercy for us, have Mercy on us and on the whole world."

+Evening Prayer. This could be your daily rosary or some other practice, perhaps Scripture reading.

+Your daily prayers could even be the more formal prayer of the Church known as the Liturgy of the Hours (also known as the Divine Office.) There are two versions: the four-volume version and a single-volume abridged version called "Christian Prayer."

On a final note for this chapter, I cannot recommend enough the "basic text" of the Matt Talbot Way to Sobriety, entitled: "To Slake A Thirst: The Matt Talbot Way to Sobriety," by Philip Maynard. See "Appendix G."

Appendix A: Should a Catholic attend AA meetings? I heard they're bad...

This Appendix is an edited and expanded version of a reply to a question in a Group on Facebook I was in. A member posed the following: "Should Catholics attend AA meetings? I heard they're bad..." and went on with their fears and anxieties about attending AA.

Attending AA meetings is fine as long as you remain strong in your Faith, study it, and seek out the resources the Church offers to strengthen you against temptations to drink (as well as other inordinate desires.) Most Catholics who bash AA (apart from not completely knowing what they are talking about) are unaware of the Catholic assistance and influence that existed in early AA; the 12 Steps were developed with the help of a Catholic priest who noted their similarity to the Spiritual Exercises of St. Ignatius. Also, they are loosely written enough to apply to people of all religious and spiritual traditions. Anyone can very easily reinterpret the ambiguous spirituality according to their own perspective. This means that you can Catholicize everything.

"But they mention a 'Higher Power!!' A 'God of my understanding'!!! That's pagan! New Age!!!"

"No, it isn't. Those are just generic terms for any power that the member regards as being superior to them. If they are Believers, then that is most likely God. AA is not a religion and does not impose specific religious beliefs; hence the vague generic terms for what anyone can just translate to as "God" according to whatever religion they follow, or don't follow. An atheist may regard the AA Home Group they belong to as their Higher Power. Theology, belief, or non-belief are extraneous issues when you are a drunk seeking sobriety. No one is going to force you to leave Jesus or the Catholic Church to be a member of AA, although I admit this does happen but that's incidental and likely the result of the person being weak in their faith rather because of any targeted proselytization. And the whole thing about "being weak in their faith" is central to why I started SoberCatholic.com in the first place. More on that later.

My Higher Power is Jesus. There are probably more pagans and non-Christians who are alcoholics than there are followers of Jesus and this just accommodates them. It also originally accommodated Christians of differing denominations. Just switch "Higher Power" to Jesus and be kind to everyone else. Everyone is on a spiritual journey; who knows how the Holy Spirit leads others to the Truth? Sobriety isn't just for Christians and if this "Higher Power" concept helps a pagan or atheist become sober, then so be it. You'd rather they remain a drunk and kill someone in a driving accident? Of course not. Christians can call this Higher Power "Jesus," Muslims can call it "Allah," and Hindus can refer to it as "Vishnu" or whatever.

This fear of a term is self-defeating and a distraction to the specific goal of becoming sober. I also think it is an excuse cloaked in piety to avoid taking responsibility and getting help, or maybe avoiding any perceived stigma about going to AA meetings. But AA is not the only recovery program out there; if you can find help outside of AA, great! Maybe try the Matt Talbot Way to Sobriety (See

Chapter 18) or this "Sober Catholic Way!" The only thing that matters is getting sober; how you do it is irrelevant. Even AA believes that!

AA is not about converting people to New Age paganism. It is about getting people sober. AA does not care what religion you profess or don't profess. Individual Home Groups here and there may reflect the local cultural attitudes towards Catholicism which may be supportive, indifferent, or prejudicial. If that becomes a problem for you, relocate if and when you can, or turn to online recovery. Online recovery, whether via social networks, discussion forums, or video conferencing, makes it easy to avoid local difficulties, as well as keeping you somewhat better insulated against non-Catholic spirituality.

So, yes, I am aware that AA can be a problem. Any organization made up of humans can be a problem. I'm just speaking out against the uninformed prejudice of people. I am no advocate for AA; I attended and eventually found it more uncomfortable than useful, and left. But I found a replacement and I still find some elements of AA useable. I pick and choose.

Try my advice, I have been sober (so far) since May 22, 2002, and also have been blogging at SoberCatholic.com since January 2007, so I do have a track record. If you have a problem with alcohol, go to AA. Do the "90 meetings in 90 days" plan. This is going to 90 AA meetings in 90 days. In doing "the 90 in 90" you will be exposed to anything you'll ever hear about alcoholism from AA's perspective for pretty much every life situation that people once needed to drink over. Then decide whether you wish to continue. (I advise sticking with AA for a year if you can, then go as needed or not at all.)

During your "90 in 90" make sure you get the basic literature, and I recommend the following:

-the "Big Book," aka "Alcoholics Anonymous." As of this writing, the current edition of the Big Book is the 4th, but I understand that a 5th edition is in the works and may even be out depending on when you are reading this.

- the "12 and 12" aka the "The Twelve Steps and Twelve Traditions." This is a collection of essays written by Bill Wilson, AA's co-founder, on AA's Twelve Steps of Sobriety and the Twelve Traditions by which AA is governed.

-the book "Experience, Strength, and Hope," which contains personal stories from earlier editions of the Big Book that are no longer included in the current edition.

-"Daily Reflections" is a collection of 366 daily meditations written by alcoholics for alcoholics.

-"Living Sober" is another essential book, containing essays for sober living. It's just advice gleaned from AA meetings and other AA literature for keeping sober in many situations.

-I would also like to include "As Bill Sees It," a collection of thoughts and excerpts from the writings of Bill Wilson.

-All of these can be ordered from Alcoholics Anonymous or obtained through a local AA meeting. Just ask around for the literature person. For non-AA literature, I recommend titles from Hazelden Publishing. (See Appendix G.) I'll refrain from suggesting specific titles, though.

"But, some of the stories and stuff are written by people who are…"

"So what? Take what's useful and leave the rest. 'Those people' just might say THAT ONE THING you need to hear that will keep you from the drink. Jesus dined with hookers and government types, are you better than Him?"

While I no longer attend AA meetings (but do participate in online recovery,) in-person meetings are useful and helpful as far as they go for those who need them. But there is hope for you: if in the end you have tried AA and found it wanting for whatever reason, there are options and alternatives to AA. It's up to you to find them as I've no experience with any except for the path I have trodden, which is outlined in this book you are reading.

I sobered up in the rooms of AA, but have not been a regular meeting goer since 2004. Since then it had been only "when I need a meeting." But as of this writing, my last live, face-to-face meeting was in 2014. So, AA "isn't needed," but you do need to be deep in the Church and sacraments. However, I did find that my Catholic re-interpretation of AA's spirituality was essential and invaluable. Everything just gets filtered through my Catholic lens.

Regarding attacks on AA: There is lots of misinformation out there from people with an axe to grind. Perhaps they (or someone they know) were hurt by AA (no organization made up of people is perfect, we're all sinners and things can get out of control and our Fallen Nature has a greater impact at times other than when our nature invigorated by grace. Even the Church has hurt people. No reason to leave it. Although it's understandable that people do, at least for a while.)

But I've seen irresponsible sites accusing AA of being pagan, New Age, a cult, and all sorts of things. It can be, but that might be just local conditions here and there. There was a document from Rome put out in the early 2000s listing Twelve Step movements as being damaging; it was obvious that the writer knew nothing about AA; the work was poorly researched (at least as to including AA. Spot on about other things.)

But in general, AA (or any 12 Step Group) isn't a threat to anyone's Catholicism if their Faith is deep, and if it isn't like I've already said, they should apply themselves to learning the Faith with the same dedication they apply themselves to learning the 12 Steps. After you've gotten them down and learned to live by them, they make a nice accompaniment to living by the Gospel and Beatitudes and taking part in the sacramental life of the Church. Subordinate to the tools of Faith, but still essential.

So, that is it: try AA. Learn the basics of Twelve Step living. Get the books I mentioned above and refer to them when you need something directly applicable to alcoholism. Attend meetings if and when you need them. Try online recovery. Keep increasing your knowledge of Catholicism at the same time; attend Mass (daily, if possible), study the Catechism, boost your prayer life, and frequent the sacraments (especially the Eucharist and Confession.) After you've done your "90 in 90," then decide if AA is for you.

It comes down to this:

"You shall know them by their fruits." (Matthew 7:16)

Are you sober? This doesn't mean "just not drinking." Drinking was a crutch to help you cope. Many people drink to relieve the burdens of life, but those afflicted with alcoholism are different and the crutch becomes an instrument of pain and torture rather than a support. Take away the crutch, and what have you got? The problems that afflicted you are still there; perhaps those directly attributable to your drinking will vanish, but others remain. How will you handle them? AA helps you cope with life without the crutch of the drink. If you won't use AA to whatever extent you make of it, then what will you use? Does it directly address how to stop drinking and how to live without it?

Time for a self-assessment: If you stopped drinking and did not replace it with another "life aid," how are things going? If you're irritable, restless, discontented, angry, bitter, resentful, mean-spirited, and bad-tempered, whatever you're doing isn't working. If you need confirmation, just ask your family, friends, and co-workers. They'll enjoy the opportunity to finally tell you...

Just "not drinking" isn't enough, you have to find something that "reprograms" you and helps you react to things in a civil and socially acceptable manner without resorting to the drink to help. Again, Matthew 7:16. What are the fruits of your "program" of recovery from alcoholism if you do not attend AA? Again, you needn't attend AA meetings for the rest of your life as many believe, but some basic education in the Twelve Steps is invaluable.

Appendix B: Can a recovered alcoholic drink wine at Mass?

While the wine is transubstantiated by the priest during Mass, it still retains the properties of alcohol.

The Church teaches that the entirety of the Real Presence of Christ, that being His Body, Blood, Soul, and Divinity are found in the transubstantiated bread. Therefore there is no reason at all for an alcoholic of any length of sobriety to receive the Eucharist in the form of wine.

Appendix C: What are dogmas and doctrines? I heard they're straitjackets restricting our freedom!

The terms "dogma" and "doctrine" are often bandied about as pejoratives by people who do not know what they mean. For those who are non-religious, they imply being "chained" or "oppressed" by rigid religious beliefs. This is utter nonsense.

If you look up both words in a reliable Catholic source, a "dogma" is simply a Truth about God. These dogmas are described in the Apostles and Nicene Creeds. A dogma is an aspect of who or what God is. Doctrines are merely the teachings of the Church.

There are also Marian dogmas. Currently four in number, they are:

+Mary's Divine Maternity (she is the Mother of God)

+Her perpetual virginity (she retained her virginity before, during, and after Christ's conception)

+Her Assumption into Heaven (she did not suffer the corruption of death. Whether she died or not is subject to interpretation, the Eastern Churches refer to her as having "fallen asleep" when she was called home to the Lord. What is referred to as the Assumption of the Blessed Virgin Mary by the Roman Catholic Church is called "Dormition" by the Greek Catholic Churches and the Orthodox Churches. That is, a falling asleep. Either way, she either didn't die or upon the time of it was bodily taken up into Heaven. Her body never suffered the corruption of death. There are mystical writings based on apparitions, such as those of the Blessed Virgin to the Ven. Maria de Jesus of Agreda, in which she reported that after the Blessed Mother died, her body did remain in her tomb for three days, just to follow the example of her Son. But her body still did not suffer death's corruption.

+Her Immaculate Conception. In 1854, Pope Pius XI proclaimed in Ineffabilis Deus the following:

> We declare, pronounce, and define that the doctrine which holds that the most Blessed Virgin Mary, in the first instance of her conception, by a singular grace and privilege granted by Almighty God, in view of the merits of Jesus Christ, the Saviour of the human race, was preserved free from all stain of original sin, is a doctrine revealed by God and therefore to be believed firmly and constantly by all the faithful.

This latter dogma makes sense on many different levels. Please excuse me as I go way off this book's subject matter and defend Mary's Immaculate Conception. However, if you take a look at it, it could very well apply to the Sober Catholic Way (meaning why its practitioners should develop a devotion to Our Lady's Immaculate Conception.)

God exists outside of time and is not restricted by the chronological sequence of events that occur within time.

The Holy Spirit could not have 'overshadowed' Mary to form Jesus in her womb if she was in the state of Original Sin. Mary's union with the Holy Spirit is a spousal union. "What God had joined, let none rend asunder." This is an important point that helped me finally understand more solidly the whole 'Immaculate Conception' thing. Her spousal union with the Holy Spirit and the Spirit's 'overshadowing' Mary required her to be sinless. Not just preserved from Original Sin, but also the stain it leaves behind (concupiscence.) Sin blocks grace from the soul; mortal sin is deadly and separates us from God, while venial sin distances us from God. Mary's spousal union with the Spirit would have been ruptured if she was capable of sinning. Remember: "What God had joined, let none rend asunder." If she was in any state of sin, the Holy Spirit could not have joined with her in the first place.

Therefore, how can the Holy Spirit's spousal union with Mary be maintained at all if she had concupiscence? It couldn't. Therefore, Mary could not have Original Sin, and by not being subjected to it or having its stain on her soul, she was incapable of committing venial and mortal sins. This is where all other humans differ from Mary. Although by Baptism we've had Original Sin removed, its stain remains, and by this concupiscence, we sin. With Mary, since the stain was removed concupiscence was never a part of her being. But while Christians have received the Holy Spirit in Baptism, our union with the Spirit is not to the same degree as Mary's. Ours is not a spousal union; sin can rupture it. Hence, we need the Sacraments to repair the rupture.

Since she bore Him in her womb for nine months, she could not even commit venial and mortal sins during this period as this would place Jesus under the domain of Satan, since a fetus is physically a part of the mother. (While not culpable for the mother's sins, nor capable of sinning itself, a fetus would still be affected by them.) Her sinless behavior obviously would have continued after Jesus' birth. This is the basis for the teachings of Sts. Lous de Montfort and Maximilian Kolbe when they wrote that Mary's will was always in conformity with God's will. Kolbe especially emphasized this.

So, the Dogma of the Immaculate Conception has the effect also of rendering the rubrics of administering the sacraments more meaningful, given the role of the Holy Spirit in everything. The Spirit joined with Mary because she was without sin. We are baptized and Original Sin is removed and then the Holy Spirit enters our soul and later we can receive the remaining sacraments.

Some critics point out that St. Paul said somewhere in his letters that "all have sinned." Well, this cannot possibly mean 'all' as in 'everyone;' for would this 'all' include Jesus? I think Paul meant 'all born of women' in the normal manner of birthing. If someone is still going to make the point that 'all' inherit Original Sin, and then Mary would still need redeeming, then we go back to the original declaration of the dogma of her immaculate conception that she was redeemed by the anticipated merits of Jesus Christ and so was prevented from having the stain of Original Sin in the first place. (Please refer to the first point for any chronological objections.)

"…wouldn't God, Who knew from all Eternity His plan of Salvation, and decided that His Son would be born of a woman rather than Incarnate as a mighty king and lord fully grown, wouldn't He have taken great pains to decide upon the formation of she who would bear His Son?" If YOU had the opportunity to design your own mother, wouldn't YOU insist that she the among the most beautiful, intelligent, and talented of all? One of the Ten Commandments holds that we should "Honor our Father and Mother," well, wouldn't God also follow that? Even if one were to declare that He is not subject to His Commandments and laws, why wouldn't He follow that one at least, to provide an example?" An addendum to this point is that if YOU could make your own mother, and could also make her perfectly pure and holy, wouldn't you?

"…One could argue then that why couldn't Jesus have been conceived immaculately?" He could have, but the difficulty in that would be that He still would be in Mary's womb, and what would be the barrier between Him and Original Sin? His sacrifice on the cross, decades later? He is divine and sinless, so His death was not for Himself, He died for humanity. So Mary, by sharing her body and blood with Jesus in her womb, would benefit from the eventual sacrifice of Jesus. Mary is the physical barrier between Jesus and her ancestral line, caught in Original Sin like the rest of humanity. The physical barrier protecting Mary from her mother's state of Original Sin was Jesus, operating from the fullness of time, as God dwells in Eternity.

So, there it is! See how it all connects? Remove Original Sin and the free operation of the Holy Spirit can begin in souls. With Mary, it required her to be preserved from all sin so the Holy Spirit could join her in an eternal spousal union so that Jesus could be formed in her. With us, it required us to be Baptized so the Holy Spirit could join us in a sacramental union so that we could be formed into the Mystical Body of Christ.

Appendix D: The Corporal and Spiritual Works of Mercy

The corporal works of mercy:

To feed the hungry;

To give drink to the thirsty;

To clothe the naked;

To shelter the homeless;

To care for the sick;

To ransom the captive/visit the imprisoned

To bury the dead.

The spiritual works of mercy:

To instruct the ignorant;

To counsel the doubtful;

To admonish sinners;

To bear wrongs patiently;

To forgive offenses willingly;

To comfort the afflicted;

To pray for the living and the dead.

Appendix E: A Triduum of Marian Consecrations

This is a devotional practice I am suggesting that builds upon existing devotions. There are already people devoted to consecrating themselves to Our Lady of Fatima every month on the 13th. I found an old devotional booklet suggesting the same to Our Lady of Guadalupe on the 12th of every month. I decided that Our Lady of Lourdes (on the 11th of the month) should be included, given the importance of that title of Our Lady to anyone recovering from alcoholism and other addictions.

The consecutive days of the 11th (since Our Lady appeared to St. Bernadette on February 11, 1858,) the 12th (as the miraculous image on the tilma of St. Juan Diego appeared on the 12th of December, 1531), and the 13th (as The Blessed Mother appeared on the 13th of the month from May to October, 1917 in Fatima, Portugal) all flow together in a nicely symbolic way. You may recall that I mentioned in the chapter on Fatima that Fatima steps in if the messages of Guadalupe and Lourdes aren't heeded.

Our Lady of Lourdes is associated with healing. Spiritual healing, physical healing, all sorts of healing. Seventy of the medical ones have been declared miraculous (out of the over seven thousand reported.) Our Lady also told the seer, St. Bernadette Soubirous, messages concerning repentance from sin.

Our Lady of Guadalupe can help us appreciate our dignity as children of God, across racial and cultural divisions. She calls for the unity of peoples. In rejecting the objectification of others, our humanity is made manifest to us and we reject drugs and alcohol.

Our Lady of Fatima is a call to "Prayer, Conversion and Penance." These are the core attributes of the Sober Catholic Way (or, better yet, the Matt Talbot Way!)

So, please try and do this every month. It takes but a few minutes every day.

Act of Consecration to Our Lady of Lourdes
(to be said every month on the 11th):
Holy Mary, Mother of God, Virgin Immaculate, you appeared 18 times to Bernadette at the grotto in Lourdes to remind Christians of what the truths in the Gospel require of them. You call them to prayer, penance, the Eucharist and the life of the church. To answer your call more fully, I dedicate myself, through you, to your Son Jesus. Make me willing to accept what he said. By the fervor of my faith, by the conduct of my life in all its aspects, by my devotion to the sick, let me work with you in the comforting of those who suffer and in the reconciliation of people that the church may be one and there be peace in the world. All this I ask, confident that you, Our Lady, will fully answer my prayer. Blessed be the Holy and Immaculate Conception of the Blessed Virgin Mary, Mother of God. Our Lady of Lourdes, pray for us. St. Bernadette, pray for us.

And so today, may Mary, the Mother of God, the Immaculate Conception, Our Lady of Lourdes intercede for us and lead us closer to her son, Jesus.

Act of Consecration to Our Lady of Guadalupe

(to be said every month on the 12th):

O most Holy Virgin Mary, Mother of God, I (Name,) although most unworthy of being thy servant, yet moved by thy wonderful mercy and by my desire to serve thee, consecrate myself to thy Immaculate Heart, and choose thee today, in the presence of my Guardian Angel and the whole heavenly court, for my especial Lady, Advocate and Mother, under the title of Our Lady of Guadalupe, the name given to the heavenly image left us as pledge of they motherly kindness. I firmly resolve that I will love and serve thee always, and do whatever I can to induce others to love and serve thee. I pray thee, Mother of God, and my most kind and amiable Mother, that thou wilt receive me into the number of thy servants for thy child and servant forever. Assist me in all my thoughts, words, and actions at every moment of my life, that every step and breath be directed to the greater glory of God; and through thy most powerful intercession obtain for me that I may never more offend my beloved Jesus, that I may glorify Him in this life, and that I may also love thee, and enjoy thee, in the company of the Blessed Trinity through eternity in holy Paradise.

In order to live this consecration as another St. Juan Diego, I promise to renew it frequently, especially on the twelfth day of each month; and mindful of thy messages to us at Lourdes and Fatima, I will strive to lead a life of prayer and sacrifice, of fidelity to thy Rosary and of reparation to thy Immaculate Heart. Amen.

Act of Consecration to Our Lady of Fatima

(to be said every month on the 13th):

O Most Holy Mary, Virgin Mother of God, Queen of Heaven and Earth, in accordance with thy wish made known at Fatima, I consecrate myself today to thine Immaculate Heart. To thee I entrust all that I have, all that I am, to thy blessed charge and special keeping and into thine Immaculate Heart. For this day, for every day of my life, and at the hour of my death, I commend my soul and body.

To thee do I entrust all my hopes and consolations, all my trials and miseries, my life and the end of my life, that through thy most holy intercession and thy merits all my actions may be ordered and disposed according to thy will, and that of thy Divine Son.

Reign over me dearest Mother, that I may be thine in prosperity, in adversity, in health and in sickness, in life and in death. Grant that I may have no other spirit but thy spirit, to know Jesus Christ and His Divine and Holy Will; that I may have no other soul but thy soul, to praise and glorify the Lord; that I may have no other heart but thy heart, to love God with a pure and burning love like thine.

My beloved Mother, my glorious Queen, I am all thine and all that I have is thine. Amen.

Appendix F: "Recovering Catholics" and "Spiritual but not Religious"

This deals with two issues that have repeatedly irked me over the time I've been in recovery. Although they are two separate subjects, they are related as they have one thing in common: animosity or skepticism towards organized religion and especially the Catholic Church.

They are the phrase "Recovering Catholic" and people who are "Spiritual but not Religious."

First up is "Recovering Catholic."

I encounter that phrase quite a lot in social media and online recovery groups.

As you must have realized by now from reading this book and especially if you've been a reader of SoberCatholic.com for any amount of time, my Faith has been extremely important to me in my recovery from alcoholism. My Catholicism is tightly wrapped up in my experience, strength, and hope.

When I do a search in online recovery groups for "Catholic," I usually find a bunch of people.

And often the word "Catholic" is right after the word "Recovering."

To me, that term is mean-spirited and hurtful. It also means that the people identifying themselves as "Recovering Catholics" have unresolved issues with the Church. What do 12 Step programs say about such things? I forget the exact quote in AA's "Big Book," but there is something in it about how anger and resentment are two things that alcoholics (and by modern extension, any addict) cannot afford.

They are dangerous landmines. These unresolved issues are just waiting to bite you and perhaps be the trigger for a relapse. Any resentment or unresolved issue needs to be addressed regardless of how uncomfortable it is or how "satisfying" it makes you feel.

Why the term "Recovered (or "Recovering") Catholic" anyway? Catholicism is an ancient and deep religion and spirituality that has been one of the primary architects of Western civilization. There is much within it that is useful to anyone in recovery. If a person has been harmed by the Church, whether by abuse (of any kind), or they were raised "too strict," or they have difficulties with the Church's teachings, all these need to be explored and dealt with.

Regarding abuse: individuals caused it. Not the Church as an institution. Granted, the Church has badly handled the clerical sexual abuse crisis. Those who abused, or who covered up the abuse and did other wrongs will eventually suffer just punishments. I am by no means soft-pedaling a serious and critical issue. But the lasting anger and resentment that victims feel years later are hardly a "healing." There are resources available within the Church and outside it that can assist people in healing from abuse. It may take years, but the process should be started, and take as long as it takes. Otherwise, you're never completely "recovered" from what happened.

If they were raised by "too strict" parents (or taught by nuns who were too "tough"), so what? That was the parent's or nun's fault. Why did they feel so strongly about the Faith that they drove it home so hard? Perhaps they saw how secular society was corrosive and felt this was the only way to insulate you from it. Perhaps you can learn from authentic and legitimate Catholic sources as to what the Church teaches, and more importantly why She teaches that. Your eyes, heart, and mind may be opened. To tell you the truth, I was raised Catholic by my parents, my father was rather strict (less so with me than with my much older siblings). But I had enough and left the Church. I wandered about a spiritual desert for maybe 15 years before returning. I am grateful that I did. The Church saved my life. Maintaining a harsh attitude against the Church for how Her teachings were inculcated in you is hardly a sign of one in a good recovery (from an addiction. Again that "resentment" word.)

If it is difficulty with Church teachings, then the same advice: learn from authentic and legitimate Catholic sources as to what the Church teaches, and more importantly why. You may come to understand.

This all takes honesty, open-mindedness, and willingness. It also takes humility.

Many people in recovery find their religious faith (Catholic or otherwise) to be of immense help. Going 12 Step-only does not always work (see "Preface,") many people need something more. To identify yourself in a manner that bashes another religion is counterproductive and just plain impolite. It is harmful to others; particularly those of that Faith to whom it may be important, and ultimately paints yourself as an individual who may have a shaky recovery (no matter how long sober and clean.)

If you cannot fully deal with and resolve issues from your past, then how can you be of help to others?

The point is, that no matter what the reason is for a person's use of the term "Recovering Catholic," it does signify something that needs to be addressed and resolved. Something deep inside is still hurting. Honesty and humility are useful tools in doing this. You may not ever return to the Catholic Church, but perhaps the hate, anger, and resentment will fade.

Forgiveness and perhaps even reconciliation are ultimately needed. Many "in the rooms" say the Lord's Prayer during meetings, or on their own. You may want to take a look at the line towards the end:

"And forgive us our trespasses as we forgive others who trespass against us."

It means that God will not forgive you of your sins against Him or others unless you also forgive others of their sins against you. It is tough. Forgiveness may be the toughest thing anyone can do. If it was easy, the world would be a far more peaceful place.

Some things to ponder.

Next up is "Spiritual but not religious."

"Religion" can be defined as an organized system of beliefs that order and regulate a person's or society's relationship with God or some other "deity." Religions vary a lot in their demands and expectations, but that definition should cover all of them.

"Spirituality" can be defined as something looser, perhaps an individual's or group of individual's sense of their souls and non-material existence, and the focusing of their efforts on cultivating that side of themselves.

I can see how being "spiritual but not religious" is enticing and preferable. You are essentially deciding for yourself, based on your feelings and self-will, how to relate to God or the supernatural. You are remaking God in your image and likeness.

Naturally, that is easier. Organized religions such as Catholicism impose standards of belief and behavior that may be at odds with our feelings. Religion has hurt people (recall the preceding paragraphs on "Recovering Catholics.") But if you ignore religion and just cultivate your spirituality, you probably are placing fewer burdens on yourself, or are more forgiving when you fail to live up to the demands you've established. This is not to say that all "spiritual but not religious" types avoid anything tough; I know that some follow ascetical practices that place rigorous demands on their lives. But this is still a decision of the self and can be ended whenever the person decides that. It is not a willing response to follow something originating from outside themselves that may require humility and self-discipline. Yes, you can develop a spiritual practice and impose penalties whenever you fail the standards you establish for yourself, but in general, people do not always do that.

The point I am attempting to make is this: it is wrong to think of one and not the other. To me, religion and spirituality are two sides of the same coin. They go hand in hand.

For the purposes of this book and the blog that inspired it, I will now focus on Catholicism as the "religion" in question. Religion (Catholicism) is God's reaching out to humankind through His self-revelation through the ancient prophets and patriarchs (the Hebrew Scriptures, aka "Old Testament") culminating in the advent of His Son, the Messiah; Jesus Christ (the New Testament.). In these self-revelations, we discover God and His love and mercy. We learn the correct way to worship and pray to Him. In doing all this, we learn about ourselves as we respond to His self-revelation. That response is "spirituality."

Taking the definition of spirituality above and applying it in this manner, we can modify that definition this way: "Spirituality" is an individual's or group of individual's personal sense of their souls and non-material existence, and focusing these efforts at cultivating that side of themselves by adhering to God's self-revelation and His expectations of us. God made us; we did not will ourselves into being. Therefore, God is entitled to define the boundaries of our relationship with Him.

Religion is God's reaching out to us and spirituality is our response to that.

Religion (Catholicism) provides a unifying set of beliefs that brings a sense of order out of the chaos of secular culture. Religion (Catholicism) is shared by all members, but the spirituality may be diverse. How each Catholic responds to the demands of Catholicism varies according to the individual. I am not referring to the degree to which Catholics accept the Church's teachings, although that is a factor in a person's spirituality. I am referring to the diverse devotions and charisms of the Faith. (Charisms being the various religious orders and their spirituality and the ability of Catholics to participate in them.) And devotions are, well, if you've gotten this far in the book, then you know quite a lot of them!

Religion without spirituality is merely rules and regulations; the Pharisaical dimension of the faith. Spirituality without religion is often the lowest common denominator system of beliefs. While well-meaning, spirituality without religion lacks the self-discipline and sacrifices religion requires. Religion offers a roadmap to God designed by God Himself. Spirituality offers roadmaps designed by people who often know not where the destination is (although they would disagree with this, of course.)

Religion strengthens spirituality and provides direction and courage for when things get hard (recall that parable of Jesus about the guy who built his house on a foundation of rock versus the one who didn't.) Spirituality prevents religion from being just a harsh and unforgiving taskmaster.

Religion and spirituality go hand in hand, each one correcting the flaws and problems of the other.

Appendix G: Resources on Recovery

This Appendix lists the resources referred to in each chapter.

Preface: All Scripture quotes are courtesy of the "Sacred Bible: Catholic Public Domain Version." The website is http://www.sacredbible.org/catholic/index.htm

More about me: https://www.sobercatholic.com/paulcoholic/

I: Go to Mass and live the Sacramental life of the Church

and

II: Adore Jesus in the Blessed Sacrament

St. Alphonsus Ligouri; Visits To The Blessed Sacrament and the Blessed Virgin Mary, abridged edition; 2002; TAN Books

https://www.therealpresence.org/eucharst/a.html

https://www.catholic.com/encyclopedia/eucharist

https://www.catholic.com/encyclopedia/sacraments

III: Study the Bible (Make sure it's a Catholic one!)

Good Catholic Bibles:

I won't get into details about each bible, like the translation methods, such as 'dynamic equivalence,' 'formal equivalence' and so forth; or other things that get traditionalists and modernists all a-twitter. You can research the nitty-gritties on your own. I like them all and use them depending on the situation I'm in and my mood. I'll just write a little bit on each as if I were speaking with you across a table drinking something non-alcoholic. All of these are fine and safe for Catholics.

Douay-Rheims (DR). Really old and traditional Catholic Bible from the late 1700s. The original one was made in the late 16th and early 17th Century and translated from the Latin Vulgate Bible of St. Jerome. It was made so that English Catholics, neck-deep in being persecuted by the Anglican Church and British Crown, can have a safe, non-King James Version Bible. Solidly orthodox and faithful. Lots of 'thees' and 'thous,' words ending in -eth, and other archaic word usage. I like it when I want to really feel old-school traditional.

Jerusalem Bible (JB). 1960s English version of a French Bible that was translated from the original sacred languages of Hebrew, Aramaic, and Greek. I like it because it reads well and it was favored by Mother Angelica of EWTN. If you watch her old shows the bible she carries with "WORD OF GOD" emblazoned on the front is this one. (The "Word of God" is a special cover sold by EWTN you can fit over your JB.) Oh, before I forget, there are *two editions* of the JB. The Standard (or Regular) Edition has copious, detailed explanatory notes. The Reader's Edition has an abridged version of the notes. (Mother Angelica used the Reader's Edition.) The Standard Edition is hard to find; I got mine in a used book sale. It is very good for lectio divina.

Knox Bible. 1950s English Bible single-handedly translated from the Latin Vulgate Bible of St. Jerome by Fr. Ronald Knox. A good, easy read with interesting perspectives on traditional verses ('interesting' does not imply heterodoxy. The Ven. Bishop Fulton Sheen favored this version.) If you like reading JRR Tolkien, GK Chesterton, Hilaire Belloc, and other English Catholic writers of the early/mid-20th Century, you'll enjoy this. It is very good for lectio divina.

New American Bible (NAB). The official Bible of the Catholic Church in the United States and translated from the original sacred languages of Hebrew, Aramaic, and Greek. The Mass readings are based on it, so it's probably familiar to you. It succeeded the older Confraternity Version (CV) of the Bible which had been translated from the Latin Vulgate Bible of St. Jerome. (If you can find the CV in used bookstores or left behind in a corner of a Catholic Church where people leave things for others to take, get it.) I use the original 1970 version of the NAB since it was a present to me from my parents on my 21st birthday. The current version has the 2010 Old Testament and Psalms and the 1986 New Testament. I understand that a newer translation of the New Testament is due out sometime in the mid/late 2020s.

New Catholic Bible. Translated from the original sacred languages and authorized by the Philippine Bishop's Conference. It reads like the NAB.

Revised Standard Version-Catholic Edition (RSV-CE). 1960s English Bible translated from the original sacred languages. It's a 'Catholicized' version of an earlier Protestant Bible, the Revised Standard Version. It is very good for lectio divina. I recall Fr. Benedict Groeschel (who wrote quite a lot of books that would be useful to sobering Catholics,) and who had a lot of programming on EWTN, favored this.

Revised Standard Version-Second Catholic Edition (RSV-2CE). Early 2000s update of the RSV-CE. It seems to be highly favored by many of the contemporary Catholic evangelizers and apologists on EWTN and other Catholic radio and TV outlets. Also good for Lectio Divina.

Lectio Divina:

https://saintandrewsabbey.com/homily/accepting-the-embrace-of-god-the-ancient-art-of-lectio-divina/

IV: Study the Catechism

Council of Trent; Catechism of the Council of Trent; 2009; TAN Books

Libreria Editrice Vaticana; Catechism of the Catholic Church, Revised; 2023; Our Sunday Visitor Press

V: Read the "Imitation of Christ" by Thomas a Kempis

Thomas À Kempis (Author), Richard Challoner (Translator); The Imitation of Christ; 2005; Baronius Press (NOTE: This same version, 'the Challoner version' is published by TAN Books. Challoner is the same person who updated the DR in the late 1700s)

VI: Devotion to the Sacred Heart of Jesus and the Immaculate Heart of Mary.

Anne Costa; Healing Promises: The Essential Guide to the Sacred Heart; 2017; Franciscan Media

Anne Costa; A Little Book of Reparation: First Friday Devotion of the Sacred Heart of Jesus; 2022; (self-published)

Fr. John Croiset, SJ; Devotion to the Sacred Heart of Jesus: How to Practice the Sacred Heart Devotion; 2007; TAN Books.

Mary C. Darrah; Sister Ignatia: Angel of Alcoholics Anonymous, Second Edition; 2001; Hazelden.

Fr. Gnarocas; Seemingly Impossible, but True! The Nine First Fridays; 1996; One Hundred One Foundation

Fr. Nicholas A. Norman; Consecration to the Immaculate Heart of Mary; 1988; TAN Books

VII: Say the Rosary Every Day

St. Louis De Monfort; The Secret of the Rosary; 2018; Martino Fine Books

St. Louis De Monfort; The Secret of Mary; 1998; TAN Books

Paul Sofranko; The Recovery Rosary: Reflections for Alcoholics and Addicts, 2012; self-published https://www.paulsofranko.net/my-books/

VIII: Consecrate Yourself to Mary

St. Louis De Monfort; True Devotion to Mary: with Preparation for Total Consecration; 2010; TAN Books

Luigi Faccenda; One More Gift: Total Consecration to the Immaculata According to the Spirituality of St. Maximilian Kolbe, 2nd edition; 1991; Ignatius Press

Fr. Anselm Romb; Total Consecration to Mary: A Nine-day Preparation for Individuals or Groups in the Spirit of St. Maximilian Kolbe, 3rd edition; 2004; Marytown Press

Paul Sofranko, The Catholicpunk Manifesto, 2023; self-published. https://www.paulsofranko.net/my-books/ (NOTE: I wrote this as a kind of manual to apply one's consecration. It is directed at Catholic creatives and exhorts them to apply their faith to their creative works. It draws heavily on Kolbean consecration.)

Also: the Militia of the Immaculata has a lot of resources. Site: https://militiaoftheimmaculata.com or http://missionimmaculata.com

MI National Center Office

P.O. Box 5547

Peoria, IL 61601

IX: Pray the Stations of the Cross

St. Alphonsus Ligouri; The Way of the Cross; 1995; TAN Books

Paul Sofranko; The Stations of the Cross for Alcoholics; 2012; self-published (https://www.paulsofranko.net/my-books/)

X: Read the Lives of the Saints

NOTE: Selecting a saint to learn about is a personal matter. Apart from the three books listed in this part, let the Holy Spirit guide you in finding saints to study. Some hints: the saint you were named after (assuming you were;) the saint whose name you took as your Confirmation name; the saint your childhood or current parish was named after; the patron saint of the country you live in or from where your ancestors emigrated from; the patron saint of your profession, vocation, avocation or hobby. Also, any saint who seems to come up a lot in your spiritual journey is a good one to consider. They could be picking you!

Alban Butler (Author); Herbert J. Thurston (Editor), Donald Attwater (Editor); Butler's Lives of the Saints (Volumes 1-4) Revised edition; 1956; Christian Classics

Alban Butler; Lives of the Saints; 1995; TAN Books

H Hoever; Illustrated Lives of the Saints Vols. 1 & 2 (Boxed Set); 2007; Catholic Book Publishing.

XI: Get to know St. Joseph

Anonymous; Favorite Prayers to St. Joseph; 1997; TAN Books

Pere Binet; The Divine Favors Granted To St. Joseph; 1983; TAN Books

Fr. Donald Calloway; Consecration to St. Joseph: The Wonders of Our Spiritual Father; 2020; Marian Press

Dr. Mark Miravalle, Meet Your Spiritual Father: A Brief Introduction to St. Joseph; 2015; Marian Press

Edward Healy Thompson; The Life and Glories of Saint Joseph; 1980; TAN Books

XII: Live the Beatitudes

See resources for Chapters 13-18, and Appendix D

XIII: Live the Little Way of St. Therese.

Fr. Charles Arminjon; The End of the Present World and the Mysteries of the Future Life; 2011; Sophia Institute Press

St. Therese of Lisieux (Author), Francis Broome (Translator); The Little Way for Every Day: Thoughts from Thérèse of Lisieux; 2006; Paulist Press

St. Therese de Lisieux (author), John Clarke (translator); Story of a Soul: The Autobiography of St. Therese of Lisieux, Third Edition; 1996; ICS Publications

St. Therese de Lisieux (author), Marc Foley (Author) John Clarke (translator); Story of a Soul: Study Edition; 2005; ICS Publications

Thomas à Kempis; The Imitation of Christ; 1991; TAN Books

XIV: Live the Divine Mercy Message

Fr. George W. Kosicki, CSB; Thematic Concordance To The Diary Of St. Maria Faustina Kowalska; 2001, Marian Press

Fr. George Kosicki, CSB; Why Mercy Sunday; 2017; Marian Press

St. Maria Faustina Kowalska; Divine Mercy In My Soul - Diary of Sister Maria Faustina Kowalska; 2000; Marian Press

Fr. Seraphim Michalenko, MIC; The Divine Mercy Message And Devotion; 1980; Marian Press (NOTE: Includes how to recite the Chaplet of Divine Mercy.)

Bryan Thatcher, MD; Living The Message Of Divine Mercy; 2002; Marian Press

Bryan Thatcher, MD; Divine Mercy As A Way Of Life: The Role Of Forgiveness, Trust, And Mercy In Our Lives; 2018; Marian Press

XV: Live the Message of Guadalupe

Carl Anderson, Eduardo Chavez; Our Lady of Guadalupe: Mother of the Civilization of Love; 2017; Image Books

Warren H. Carroll; Our Lady of Guadalupe and the Conquest of Darkness; 2004; Christendom Press

Donald Demarest (Editor), Coley Taylor (Editor); The Dark Virgin-Our Lady of Guadalupe; 1956; Coley Taylor, Inc

Joseph Julián González (Author), Monique González (Author); Guadalupe and the Flower World Prophecy: How God Prepared the Americas for Conversion Before the Lady Appeared; 2023; Sophia Institute Press

Fr. Miguel Guadalupe; The Seven Veils of Our Lady of Guadalupe; 2000; Queenship Publishing

Francis Johnston; The Wonder of Guadalupe: The Origin and Cult of the Miraculous Image of the Blessed Virgin in Mexico; 1993; TAN Books

Franciscan Friars of the Immaculate; A Handbook on Guadalupe; 2009, Academy of the Immaculate

Grzegorz Gorny (Author), Janusz Rosikon (Author); Guadalupe Mysteries: Deciphering the Code; 2016; Ignatius Press

Thomas Mary Sennott; Not Made By Hands: The Miraculous Images of Our Lady of Guadalupe and the Shroud of Turin; 2011; Ignatius Press

XVI: Live the Message of Lourdes

Gerald Korson (Editor), John Pepino (Translator); The Wonders of Lourdes: 150 Miraculous Stories of the Power of Prayer to Celebrate the 150th Anniversary of Our Lady's Apparition; 2008; Magnificat

René Laurentin; Bernadette Speaks: A Life of St. Bernadette Soubirous in Her Own Words; 1999; Pauline Books & Media

René Laurentin; Bernadette of Lourdes, 2nd edition; 1998; Barton, Longman & Todd Ltd;

Patricia McEachern; A Holy Life: The Writings of St. Bernadette of Lourdes; 2005; Ignatius Press

Paul Sofranko; "Harold Gomes: An Authentic Knight at the Foot Of The Cross;" The Knight of the Immaculata: e-Publication of the Militia of the Immaculata, USA, Issue 88, February 2024, p. 15-16. https://militiaoftheimmaculata.com/wp-content/uploads/2020/06/FEBRUARY-2024-e-pub-final-web.pdf

Francis Trochu; Saint Bernadette Soubirous, 1844-1879; 1958; Longmans, Green and Co.

Francois Vayne; 15 Days of Prayer With Saint Bernadette of Lourdes, Revised edition; 2009; New City Press

Marlene Watkins; Everyday Miracles of Lourdes: Twenty Extraordinary Experiences along the Way to the Grotto; 2023; EWTN Publishing

Franz Werfel; The Song of Bernadette; 2006; Ignatius Press (NOTE: Although this is a classic work on St. Bernadette and Lourdes and a great movie was made from it, the author does take some "dramatic license" in telling the story. Still, it is excellent and you have to be grateful to the author who wrote it as a votive offering after being protected from the Nazis during their occupation of France.)

XVII: Live the Message of Fatima

Renzo Allegri and Roberto Allegri; Fatima: The Story Behind the Miracles; 2002; Charis Books

Anonymous; Our Lady of Fatima's Peace Plan from Heaven; 1983; TAN Books

Fr. Andrew Apostoli C. F. R.; Fatima for Today: The Urgent Marian Message of Hope; 2012; Ignatius Press

Fr. Andrew Apostoli, CFR; Fatima And The Triumph Of Mary; 2016; Blue Army Press

Fr. Donald Calloway, MIC; How To Make The Five First Saturdays; 2018; Marian Press

Warren H. Carroll; 1917: Red Banners, White Mantle; 1981; Christendom Press

Fr. J. da Cruz; More About Fatima and the Immaculate Heart of Mary; 1979; L. Owen Traynor

Sr. Angela de Fatima Coelho; Inside the Light: Understanding the Message of Fatima; 2020; TAN Books

Grzegorz Gorny, Janusz Rosikon; Fatima Mysteries: Mary's Message to the Modern Age; 2017; Ignatius Press

Jean Heimann; Fatima: The Apparition That Changed the World; 2017; TAN Books

Francis Johnston; Fatima: The Great Sign; 2010; TAN Books

Sister Lucia (Author), Louis Kondor (Editor), Joaquin M. Alonso (Introduction), Dominican Nuns of Perpetual Rosary (Translator); Fatima in Lucia's Own Words; 2000; Secretariado dos Pastorinhos

Sister Lúcia (Author), Dominican Nuns of Perpetual Rosary (Translator); Fatima in Lucia's Own Words II; 2000; Secretariado dos Pastorinhos

Sister Lúcia (Author); Dominican Nuns of Perpetual Rosary (Translator); Calls from the Message of Fatima; 2000; Secretariado dos Pastorinhos

Joseph A. Pelletier, The Sun Danced at Fatima, Revised edition; 1983; Image Books

William T. Walsh; Our Lady of Fatima; 1954; Image Books

World Apostolate of Fatima; Spiritual Guide for the Salvation of Souls and World Peace; 2008; World Apostolate of Fatima

XVIII: Live the Matt Talbot Way

Eddie Doherty, 2nd edition (Author), Rob Huston (Editor); Matt Talbot; 2001; Madonna House

Philip Maynard; To Slake a Thirst: The Matt Talbot Way to Sobriety; 2000; Alba House (NOTE: Reissued as an ebook here: https://www.stpaulsusa.com/English/E-Books/TO-SLAKE-A-THIRST)

Mary Purcell; Matt Talbot and His Times: a New Authentic Life of the Servant of God; 2021; Hassell Street Press

Mary Purcell; Remembering Matt Talbot,2nd edition; 1990; Ignatius Press

---

Additional information on these and other topics important to sobering Catholics can be found on my blog: https://www.sobercatholic.com, such as:

Addiction and Mental Health Resources: https://www.sobercatholic.com/addiction-and-mental-health-resources/

Pro-life info and Post-Abortion Healing: https://www.sobercatholic.com/pro-life-info-and-post-abortion-healing/

How to learn more about, or return to, the Catholic Church: https://www.sobercatholic.com/come-home-to-the-catholic-church/

Marian Consecration by St. Maximilian Kolbe: https://www.sobercatholic.com/militia-of-the-immaculata-and-st-maximilian-kolbe/

Other resources:

Calix Society: https://www.calixsociety.org

Hazelden: https://www.hazelden.org

Online recovery: there are many places, I'll just name a few:

In the Rooms is a social network for people in recovery. https://www.intherooms.com The Daily Pledge is another: https://thedailypledge.org. I am on both.

The "Addiction and Mental Health Resources" page on Sober-Catholic.com lists several online resources under the "Catholic Resources for Alcoholics" (including many Matt Talbot sites. These come and go which is why I am not listing any here) and "Other Addiction Resources" lists: https://www.sobercatholic.com/addiction-and-mental-health-resources/

Facebook, MeWe, X/Twitter, Reddit, and other places also have recovery communities; some good, some bad, and many reflect the culture and therefore be forewarned.

I can be reached via email at any one of the following addresses:

sobercatholic at gmail dot com

paulcoholic at gmail dot com

paulcoholic at sobercatholic dot com

Acknowledgement

I want to show my appreciation for my lovely and talented wife,
Rose Santuci-Sofranko for her love, support and encouragement
(and for the really cool cover image.) I will love you forever anden-
sum.

About The Author

Paul Sofranko

My writing efforts so far have been blogging at "Sober Catholic" (SoberCatholic.com since 2007!) and "Paul Sofranko Space" (Paul-Sofranko.net since 2012.) I am also the author of the "Stations of the Cross for Alcoholics," and "The Recovery Rosary: Reflections for Alcoholics and Addicts," "The Catholicpunk Manifesto," and "The Sober Catholic Way."

While I focus on writing devotional booklets for Catholics who are affected by alcoholism and addictions, "The Catholicpunk Manifesto" branches out from that and is more akin to some of what I write at "Paul Sofranko Space." I am currently working on novels and shorter works in the speculative fiction genre that include exploring the Works of Mercy, the shadowy boundaries between life, death and what is beyond; and what exactly exists in that stage between awake and asleep? I am convinced that some things do lurk

out of the corner of your eye. And what does sentience and humanity (or "alienity,") mean, actually?

Books By This Author

Stations of the Cross for Alcoholics

The "Stations of the Cross for Alcoholics" is a book that is rooted in an ancient Catholic devotion. It is intended to assist Catholics and other Christians find deeper meaning in their struggles with alcoholism, by connecting the oftentimes hard road of sobriety with Jesus' suffering road to His Crucifixion. The reader sees that their old alcoholic 'self' is being led to the Cross and the joy of eventual resurrection of a new sober self can follow. Whether they are still drinking and struggling, or have been sober for many years and still have difficulties coping with sobriety, this book should help readers maintain that sobriety.

The Recovery Rosary: Reflections for Alcoholics and Addicts

"The Recovery Rosary: Reflections for Alcoholics and Addicts" takes a time-honored prayer and brings it into a useful format for people to pause and reflect on their recovery, their relationships with others, and ultimately with Jesus Himself. Whether people are still struggling with their addictions, or have been clean and sober for a few weeks or months, or many years, the reflections for each Mystery of the Rosary will help them meditate on the spiritual growth they have achieved so far. Over the years, their thoughts on each

meditation may change, depending on "where they're at" in their recovery journey.

The Catholicpunk Manifesto

The Catholicpunk Manifesto is a call to arms, or rather, a call to
pens, paintbrushes, and video cameras, for creative Catholics to take
up St. Maximilian Maria Kolbe's call to infiltrate pop culture and
help alleviate the ills that pervade contemporary society. St. Maximilian saw back in the 1920s how the use of cinema, radio, and
mass-market books was corrupting society. He thought that those
same tools could be used as a force to counter this corruption. The
Catholicpunk Manifesto tells how the teachings of the Catholic Faith
can be used to provide a road map out of our current morass and a
blueprint to build a more just and fair society constructed according
to the Gospel of Jesus Christ, the Corporal and Spiritual Works of
Mercy and other elements of traditional Catholic Social Teachings
(CST)